"I truly appreciate the way Hershfield conveys complex constructs in the simplest terms. He humanizes the disorder with just enough humor to take the edge off, but not too much to negate the pain for all those affected. Obsessive-compulsive disorder (OCD) hijacks the brain and robs a giving, selfless human being of their humanity, rendering them to a seemingly selfish and entitled individual. OCD is the diagnosis given to an individual; however, it affects those in close emotional proximity to the person diagnosed. Hershfield is able to 'cut to the chase' and not engage in endless psychobabble leaving the reader confused. Quite honestly, I find it a must-read for family and friends involved with someone diagnosed with OCD."

> —**Shana Doronn, LCSW, PsyD**, doctor of psychology in the
> Obsessive-Compulsive Disorder Intensive Treatment Program
> at the University of California, Los Angeles, and featured
> therapist on A&E's *Obsessed*

"Every day at work I meet with individuals who have obsessive-compulsive disorder (OCD). I talk with their families and I try to educate them on what to do to help their family members. The families come to family sessions and I even invite them to attend an introductory talk that I give to new patients in our clinic. But those several hours of dialogue merely scratch the surface. *When a Family Member Has OCD* just made my job easier, because now there is a fantastic resource available to individuals with OCD and their families that I can recommend. I only wish I had written it. Congrats, Jon, on a major accomplishment!"

> —**Patrick B. McGrath, PhD**, clinical director of the Center
> for Anxiety and Obsessive Compulsive Disorders at Alexian
> Brothers Behavioral Health Hospital

"Families of people with obsessive-compulsive disorder (OCD) suffer, too. Reassuring doesn't help, but not reassuring can bring on rage and even destruction. Hershfield offers sound advice on this and other crucial issues, offering specifics for family members to say and do, and not to say or do. This is an excellent book for families and OCD therapists."

> —**Bruce Mansbridge, PhD**, founder of the Austin Center for
> the Treatment of OCD in Austin, TX

"With *When a Family Member Has OCD*, Jon Hershfield has produced the bible for family members to understand and better cope with their loved one's obsessive-compulsive disorder (OCD) symptoms! I will be recommending this easily understandable and compassionate book to all my patients' family members!"

—**Lee Baer, PhD**, professor of psychology in the department
of psychiatry at Harvard Medical School, and author of
Getting Control and *The Imp of the Mind*

"Within the pages of this book, Jon Hershfield offers the gift of empathic insight to families, clinicians, and researchers dealing with the complexities of obsessive-compulsive disorder (OCD). He presents both clearly researched and novel practical advice that will be accessible to a broad readership in search of wisdom on this topic. This is not a workbook, reference encyclopedia, or superficial 12-step 'solution' to the familial challenges of OCD. Rather, it brings the reader on a journey to better understand specific OCD symptoms within the family system, offering both pearls of wisdom and mountains of hope."

—**S. Evelyn Stewart, MD**, director of the pediatric OCD
program and associate professor of psychiatry at the
University of British Columbia, senior clinician scientist at
the Child and Family Research Institute, lecturer on
psychiatry at Harvard Medical School, and nonclinical
consultant in psychiatry at Massachusetts General Hospital

"*When a Family Member Has OCD* is a fantastic resource for any loved one of an obsessive-compulsive disorder (OCD) sufferer. Often the forgotten victims of OCD, families can find in this book a wealth of information not only about the illness itself, but more importantly how they can help and support their loved one in the best possible ways. This practical guide can only serve to reduce suffering for the entire family."

—**Diane Davey, RN, MBA**, program director of the
Obsessive Compulsive Disorder Institute at McLean
Hospital, a Harvard Medical School affiliate

"I communicate with obsessive-compulsive disorder (OCD) sufferers and family members of OCD sufferers all over the world who are looking for advice about what to do as the monster we know as OCD turns households upside down and rips families apart. Simply put, this book is *the* answer. It's informative, comprehensive, easily understandable, and—best of all—helpful. It should be in the hands of all those affected by this debilitating disorder, including the mental health professional community."

—**Shannon Shy**, author and OCD advocate

"A welcome and useful addition to the all-too-sparse literature available to family members of obsessive-compulsive disorder (OCD) sufferers. It is informative, compassionate, and practical, and I will certainly recommend it to my patients' families."

—**Fred Penzel, PhD**, licensed psychologist specializing in the treatment of OCD, executive director of Western Suffolk Psychological Services in Huntington, NY, and author of *Obsessive-Compulsive Disorders*

"One of the most common questions I get from the family members of my patients is, 'What am I supposed to do to help out?' I think that Jon Hershfield's book is an excellent answer to that question. He explains obsessive-compulsive disorder (OCD) in a way that is accessible to anyone, and then lays out in a very readable manner how family members should react to their loved one's illness and what role they should play during treatment. He has a unique perspective on these issues as an OCD specialist and sufferer himself, which makes the information particularly valuable to family and patients alike. I will be recommending this book to the patients in our clinic."

—**Robert Hudak, MD**, associate professor of psychiatry and medical director of the OCD Intensive Outpatient Program at the University of Pittsburgh

"Jon Hershfield brings an understanding of obsessive-compulsive disorder (OCD) based on living with the disorder combined with the knowledge and skills of a gifted therapist. The book is a great resource for family members and therapists. Family members will find an understandable, sensible approach to interacting with the person with OCD. They can learn to be helpful and supportive while not getting caught up in accommodating the OCD. I will be recommending it to family members of my patients and applying new ideas I have learned."

> —**James M. Claiborn, PhD, ABPP**, psychologist in private
> practice in Maine, diplomate of the American Board of
> Professional Psychology in Counseling Psychology, diplomate
> and founding fellow of the Academy of Cognitive Therapy,
> and member of the Scientific and Clinical Advisory Board
> of the International OCD Foundation

"Jon Hershfield masterfully balances three challenging and crucial tasks: guiding family members to greater understanding of and compassion for their loved one, educating families about how to effectively reduce/eliminate accommodation, and increasing family members' own personal mindfulness and self-care. His warmth and acceptance are apparent as he repeatedly encourages readers to invite their loved ones to collaborate in developing treatment support at home. The section on Mental Rituals paints a vivid picture of the suffering caused by unseen thought compulsions, often the hardest aspects for families to recognize and understand. Obsessive-compulsive disorder (OCD) impacts each and every family member, and Hershfield addresses this by speaking to different relationships (including parent of an adult child, sibling, spouse, or child of someone with OCD) and providing the context for the family member's experience. Families who've been thirsty for help will find this to be like a glass of cold water on a blazing day. I look forward to including this book in the orientation package for our Family Support Group members."

> —**Robin Taylor Kirk, LMFT**, executive director of
> Sage Anxiety Treatment Program

"For too long, there have not been enough informative resources for the family members of a person diagnosed with obsessive-compulsive disorder (OCD). Hershfield's *When a Family Member Has OCD* is sensitive and practical, and he speaks from his own experience. I have devoted thirty years of my career to working with families coping with the demands of OCD on how to effectively collaborate to manage the symptoms. This book is a must-read for anyone in this situation; the guidance is sound and will bring much relief to thousands of people!"

—**Barbara Van Noppen, PhD, LCSW**, Keck School of Medicine, University of Southern California

"Jon Hershfield provides a life map for families affected by obsessive-compulsive disorder (OCD). In his new book, *When a Family Member Has OCD*, [he] helps clarify the struggles families endure with their loved one diagnosed with this often debilitating illness called obsessive-compulsive disorder. Frequently, it is the family that is looking for direction and solace, and Jon Hershfield's book provides just that. Jon speaks eloquently, not only from the heart and soul of personal experience, but also from a professional perspective. A good read—clear, concise, and effective. Every family affected by OCD and every clinician helping families who are tortured by this illness should read this book!"

—**Carla Kenney, LMHC**, specialist in the treatment of OCD and other related disorders at Massachusetts General Hospital, and vice president of OCD Massachusetts, an affiliate of the International OCD Foundation (IOCDF)

"Hershfield provides a wonderful resource for clinicians and families alike. Practical, user friendly, and attuned to the needs of patients and families, the guide offers valuable advice on how to respond to some of the most common challenges posed by obsessive-compulsive disorder (OCD)."

—**Tara Peris, PhD**, assistant professor of psychiatry and biobehavioral sciences at the Semel Institute, University of California, Los Angeles (UCLA), and program director of the UCLA ABC Partial Hospitalization Program

"Hershfield gives a rich insight into understanding what obsessive-compulsive disorder (OCD) is and how it is possible to help a loved one with OCD. By synthesizing years of clinical practice with empirical research and personal experiences, this book makes the experience of OCD relatable and the treatments accessible. *When a Family Member Has OCD* is now a staple in my library and a must-read for my clients' families."

> —**Elspeth N. Bell, PhD**, licensed psychologist specializing in the treatment of OCD and hoarding disorder, in private practice in Columbia, MD

"A helpful guide in developing a collaborative, consistent, and compassionate approach in helping your family member with obsessive-compulsive disorder (OCD), while also taking care of yourself. *When a Family Member Has OCD* addresses symptoms, thoughts, and struggles common to this disorder. Practical tips are provided on how to create an atmosphere of healing in different types of family relationships. A great resource to share with my clients."

> —**Renae M. Reinardy, PsyD**, director of the Lakeside Center for Behavioral Change, and inventor of Courage Critters

"*When a Family Member Has OCD* is a must-read for anyone who has a loved one suffering from the disorder. It offers an insider's tour of the world of obsessive-compulsive disorder (OCD), as well as practical, collaborative strategies that will empower everyone in the family. Hershfield's guidance is an insightful mix of compassion, candor, and humor, and will give families the knowledge they need to provide appropriate support and assistance as their loved ones work to take back their lives from OCD."

> —**Shala Nicely**, cofounder of Beyond the Doubt

"'What about us?' 'How can we help?' Those are common questions I hear from families living with someone who has obsessive-compulsive disorder (OCD). In *When a Family Member Has OCD*, Jon Hershfield eloquently and compassionately addresses the concerns of families as he takes the reader from the early stages of identifying for the presence of OCD to diagnosis and treatment, all with a keen eye on ways to best help the family. Sensitive topics such as coping with reassurance seeking, guilt, and anger are all explored with gentleness and a subtle sense of humor which I believe readers will find both refreshing and respectful. Clearly, this book accomplishes what it sets out to do early on: it provides 'a map for navigating the key challenges of supporting and living with an OCD sufferer.' In so doing, I especially like the author's use of the 'Four I's,' as these 'steps' provide straightforward guidance in being able to put the concepts addressed into practical use. I do, however, have a suggestion for a fifth 'I'—as in, this book is an Invaluable resource for both families and professionals looking to add to their toolbox of effective coping strategies."

> —**Scott M. Granet, LCSW**, director of The OCD-BDD Clinic
> of Northern California

"This is a great resource for family members, loved ones, and friends of people who suffer from obsessive-compulsive disorder (OCD). Using his knowledge as both an OCD sufferer and a therapist, Jon Hershfield provides a detailed road map to help support the OCD sufferer with compassion and useful tools."

> —**Michelle Massi, LMFT**, licensed marriage and family therapist
> specializing in the treatment of OCD, OC-spectrum disorders,
> and anxiety disorders; and a clinical therapist at the Resnick
> Neuropsychiatric Hospital Adult OCD Intensive Treatment
> Program at the University of California, Los Angeles

"Jon Hershfield has given a gift to the obsessive-compulsive disorder (OCD) community by writing *When a Family Member Has OCD*. The book is wonderfully user friendly and is written with a warmth that is evident from page one. It is clear that the author knows OCD, and knows how to beat it. At least as important, Hershfield understands family systems and emphasizes that nothing is stronger than a family's love. This is the book I've always wanted to give to the dedicated men and women who faithfully fight alongside their loved ones with OCD."

—**Seth J. Gillihan, PhD**, clinical psychologist in Haverford, PA, and coauthor of *Overcoming OCD*

"Jon is emerging as one of the very best writers for breaking down and explaining key aspects of obsessive-compulsive disorder (OCD). He has a lucid style in conceptualizing and describing very complex issues in OCD. Jon nails certain vitally important concepts for families to understand: Did they do something to cause OCD? Is OCD curable? How do they compassionately do their part to help their family member while also keeping their family healthy and intact? He explains answers to these questions in a clear, conversational style. Jon's book has given me new ways to think about and communicate about OCD with my own patients and their family members. His book will be required reading for my undergraduate and graduate students."

—**Sarosh J. Motivala, PhD**, director of training in the OCD Adult Treatment Program at the University of California, Los Angeles, and executive director of Spectrum CBT Specialty Outpatient Clinic for OCD

"Jon Hershfield's book is an important tool in helping families understand obsessive-compulsive disorder (OCD) and, most importantly, empowering families with the knowledge and information that will help their loved ones lead a successful life with OCD."

—**Margaret Riley Sisson**, educator, advocate, Montessori School owner, board member of the Georgia affiliate of the International OCD Foundation (IOCDF), and founder of Riley's Wish Foundation, named after the son she lost to a battle with dual diagnoses of OCD and addiction

"*When a Family Member Has OCD* is a compassion-building resource that places family in the shoes of the sufferer, and hands over the key to support and understanding. Hershfield has provided an avenue for family members and sufferers to join forces against obsessive-compulsive disorder (OCD). A must-read guidebook for families and OCD sufferers alike."

> —**Stacey Kuhl Wochner, LCSW, LPCC**, psychotherapist who specializes in cognitive-behavioral therapy (CBT) for the treatment of OCD and other anxiety disorders, and founder of OCD Specialists in Los Angeles, CA

"More than just a prescriptive how-to guide, this book also provides compassionate insight into the internal experience of parents, children, siblings, and others whose loved ones have obsessive-compulsive disorder (OCD). Families will learn to shift from conflict and helplessness to collaboration and hope. I am glad to add this resource to my professional library."

> —**Amy Mariaskin, PhD**, clinical director of child and adolescent services at Rogers Behavioral Health in Nashville, TN

"I highly recommend this concise yet comprehensive guide for families who struggle to understand and live with obsessive-compulsive disorder (OCD). Written in an engaging conversational style, with examples and metaphors that bring each point home, this insightful book delivers the practical strategies that families need, along with caring and compassion for OCD sufferers and their families."

> —**Aureen Pinto Wagner, PhD**, adjunct associate professor at the University of North Carolina at Chapel Hill, and author of *Up and Down the Worry Hill, What to Do When Your Child has Obsessive-Compulsive Disorder*, and *Worried No More*

"Whether obsessive-compulsive disorder (OCD) has been an unwanted houseguest in your family's life for days or decades, Jon Hershfield's *When a Family Member Has OCD* should be a mandatory addition to your cognitive behavioral toolkit. It represents the very best of our current knowledge about OCD and is a much-needed and essential primer for any family system touched by OCD (or any therapist working to treat it effectively). Whether OCD afflicts your child, teen, adult child, parent, sibling, or friend, this book provides essential guidance on how to better understand your loved one's OCD, as well as your own efforts to cope with this complex (and often confusing) condition. Jon's writing is at its best, and his expertise, compassion, and humor blend together effortlessly with specific, practical recommendations on how to unite your family in its efforts to overcome OCD and reclaim your household."

> —**Steven J. Seay, PhD**, director of the Center for Psychological
> and Behavioral Science in Palm Beach Gardens, FL

"*When a Family Member Has OCD* is a valuable and much-needed resource educating family members and sufferers themselves on the nature of obsessive-compulsive disorder (OCD). It provides a unique and extremely accurate depiction of how it feels to live with OCD and is conveyed with honesty, compassion, and humor. It is a must-have for any family struggling with such adversities and will be certain to help each member respond to their loved one's difficulties in ways that are most conducive for the entire family system."

> —**Andrea G. Batton, LCPC**, director of The Maryland
> Anxiety Center

When a
Family Member Has
OCD

*Mindfulness & Cognitive Behavioral
Skills to Help Families Affected by
Obsessive-Compulsive Disorder*

Jon Hershfield, MFT

New Harbinger Publications, Inc.

Publisher's Note

Distributed in Canada by Raincoast Books

Copyright © 2015 by Jon Hershfield
New Harbinger Publications, Inc.
5674 Shattuck Avenue
Oakland, CA 94609
www.newharbinger.com

Cover design by Amy Shoup
Acquired by Jess O'Brien
Edited by Will DeRooy

Library of Congress Cataloging-in-Publication Data

Names: Hershfield, Jon.
Title: When a family member has OCD : mindfulness and cognitive behavioral
    skills to help families affected by obsessive-compulsive disorder / Jon
    Hershfield, MFT ; foreword by Jeff Bell.
Description: Oakland, CA : New Harbinger Publications, Inc., [2015] |
    Includes bibliographical references.
Identifiers: LCCN 2015030064| ISBN 9781626252462 (paperback) | ISBN
    9781626252479 (pdf e-book) | ISBN 9781626252486 (epub)
Subjects: LCSH: Obsessive-compulsive disorder. | Cognitive therapy. |
    Families. | BISAC: FAMILY & RELATIONSHIPS / General. | PSYCHOLOGY /
    Psychopathology / Compulsive Behavior.
Classification: LCC RC533 .H469 2015 | DDC 616.85/227--dc23 LC record available at
http://lccn.loc.gov/2015030064

Printed in the United States of America

17   16   15

10   9   8   7   6   5   4   3   2   1   First printing

To my parents, who never called me crazy

Contents

Part 3: Perspectives

Foreword

"It's time for me to do some explaining…"

Those were the first words I could think to type as I sat at my computer one afternoon in the summer of 1994, beginning what would become a long and rambling letter to my family. Just weeks earlier, I'd learned the cause of my many years of suffering, and I wanted my closest relatives to know what I now knew. I wanted them to understand my often bizarre behaviors. I wanted them to comprehend the full extent of my mental anguish. And I wanted them to appreciate how much work I had ahead of me in recovery. With the help of a stack of books I'd recently devoured, I did my best to offer my family an overview of my new diagnosis: obsessive-compulsive disorder, or OCD. Oh, how I could have used a few copies of *When A Family Member Has OCD* right then!

Years have passed since my first attempt to explain OCD to those who haven't experienced it firsthand. As a mental health advocate, I'd like to think I've gotten better at it. But, truth be told, I still struggle to convey the nuances of this complex, often baffling disorder. So much about OCD is counterintuitive, even paradoxical. Take accommodation, for example. How do we explain to loved ones that their well-intentioned efforts to reassure us may, in fact, further our challenges? Or that by allowing us to avoid our OCD triggers, they are creating an entirely new set of issues?

Jon Hershfield *gets* all this. As an OCD treatment specialist *and* an OCD survivor, Jon is uniquely qualified to help families understand both the mechanics and the hidden subtleties of this so-called doubting disease. When he first mentioned to me that he was writing this book, I knew Jon would do a terrific job with it. What I couldn't have known then was just how powerful his compilation of facts, insights, and advice would prove to be. By creating a sweeping overview of OCD—from causes, to manifestations, to treatment strategies—Jon provides families a valuable guide they can turn to again and again. But to this primer he adds something even more important: a rare "behind the curtain" look at OCD. Through recurring sections he titles "Things You Won't Observe" and "Your Family Member Might Be Concerned That…" Jon shares elucidating glimpses of life with OCD from the perspective of those who battle it.

Of the many deficiencies in that note I wrote to my family decades ago, none is more glaring than the lack of warning about how tough my OCD battles were going to be on *them*. OCD takes a huge toll on families. I know this both from my own experience and from my advocacy work. Jon knows this too, and I'm certain that's why he has gone to such great lengths to coach family members through one challenge after another that they're likely to encounter. I wish I could have armed my own loved ones with the compassionate wisdom Jon shares in these pages. I take solace in knowing that so many other families will benefit greatly from it.

—Jeff Bell
Author, *Rewind, Replay, Repeat:*
A Memoir of Obsessive-Compulsive Disorder

When a Family Member Has OCD

Introduction

Every family is a system of constantly moving parts. When one part of the system changes, it creates change in all the other parts. What this means is that when one family member experiences a mental health challenge, all family members are affected. This doesn't mean that all family members are equally affected, nor are they equally responsible for addressing the effects. However, the presence of obsessive-compulsive disorder (OCD) in any family member automatically becomes a family issue, no matter how hard the person with OCD attempts to isolate herself or shield the ones she loves from her symptoms.

OCD is a mental disorder characterized by unwanted thoughts and disruptive rituals. It drives people to behave in ways that often impair their social, academic, and professional functioning. When a family member begins behaving differently because of his OCD, it can create disruption in the family: Therapy appointments may conflict with other family members' activities. Costs of treatment may mean there's less money to spend on other things. Maybe no one can have company over if the person with OCD is having a rough day and doesn't want the extra stimulation. Furthermore, undiagnosed OCD may cause any number of conflicts around misinterpreted behavior and intentions. Every member of the family is affected in some way by the OCD. The amount of attention the disorder demands—interpersonally, financially, and time-wise—can quickly turn the family of a person with OCD into "an OCD family."

The person with OCD suffers and the OCD family suffers in different but equally meaningful ways. Yet OCD families that come together to master OCD can develop a loving interconnectedness that shines even brighter than that of families spared such adversity. The aim of this book is to function as a sort of empathy guide. In part, it's devoted to helping you understand your family member in a context that accurately represents what it's like to live with OCD. But knowing isn't really half the battle, as people say. Knowing only gets you to the battlefield. Once you're at the front lines, I hope the pages ahead can also provide you with weapons for fighting the suffering that OCD can cause not only your loved one, but also you and your whole family system.

About Me

I grew up in an OCD family. By the time I asked for help for my own OCD (around age fourteen), I was already used to hearing about "his OCD," "her OCD," "their OCD," and everybody else's OCD throughout the family tree. OCD was as common a term as anything else. I was lucky in this regard, in that the sudden barrage of horrible thoughts and the sense that my soul was being crushed every time I couldn't get something just right in my mind really came as no surprise to me. I never thought I was *crazy*. No one ever called me crazy. Maybe in all the craziness of life, no one even noticed. My father has long practiced psychiatry in a home office that had been built for him out of the side of a barn in rural Maryland. Growing up I saw mentally ill people regularly cruising up the driveway as casually as if they were coming to purchase eggs from our chickens. So asking for help came with no sense of shame. Mom sent me care packages in college with the usual— you know, mail from home, a new pair of socks, a Prozac refill. As

I got older and started asking different relatives about how their minds worked compared to mine, the common response was, "Oh, you have that too?" not "You think *whaaaaaat?!*"

When I decided to pursue a master's degree in clinical psychology, it was with one idea in mind: I wanted to do cognitive behavioral therapy for OCD. At various points in my life, I lived and breathed OCD in every waking moment, even in dreams. It seemed "Nothing ever works" and "Life is suffering" were my positive affirmations! Thankfully, cognitive behavioral therapy put me on a journey toward mastery over my OCD. At the start of that journey, I began writing to OCD discussion boards on the subject. Over time, I made fewer complaints and asked fewer questions, and instead I made more observations and offered more suggestions to my fellow sufferers. Every time I was able to help someone get the motivation to seek treatment or find the nerve to confront his fears, something clicked in my mind, suggesting that this was the right path for me. After graduate school, I worked at the OCD Center of Los Angeles, doing both individual and group therapy for adults and children with OCD, then at the UCLA Pediatric Intensive Outpatient Program, helping children and families affected by severe OCD. Today I divide my professional time between private practice, writing to the same discussion boards that helped me through the darkest times (and some new boards as well), writing blogs, and, apparently, writing books about OCD. I live and breathe OCD, but in such a different way now. The irony is not lost on me.

About This Book

This is a family guide, not a workbook, meaning I'm not going to attempt to create a comprehensive treatment plan for your family. (For a workbook-style approach, see Landsman, Rupertus, and Pedrick's 2005 book *Loving Someone with OCD: Help for You and Your Family*.) *When a Family Member Has OCD* is a map for navigating the key challenges of supporting and living with an

OCD sufferer. The purpose of this book is to shed light on what your family member is going through and how you can create a home environment conducive to better mental health for the whole family.

This book is divided into three parts. Part 1 explains the mechanics of OCD, where it comes from, what behaviors you might see (or not see) in a family member with OCD, and how it's diagnosed and treated with psychotherapy and medication. Part 2 focuses on how to understand and respond to different compulsive behaviors your family member with OCD may be engaging in. Part 3 discusses the perspectives of different family members—partners, children, parents, siblings—and offers tips and tools for balancing each family member's needs. The book concludes with an overview of ways to get help and some useful resources.

I recommend that you read this book straight through, despite the urge you may have to jump to part 3 right now to see what to do in your specific situation. Consider this: You understand your family member, because you've been around her for quite some time. You know most of her secrets—most of her quirks, unique skills, innate weaknesses, and so on. But first you had to build a foundation of more basic knowledge about her. This is true whether we're talking about someone you met as an adult (such as your partner) or a child who came into your life as a blank slate and gradually revealed his "self" to you over the years. So if you're going to truly understand your family member's OCD, you need to first establish a foundation of basic knowledge about the disorder, then meld that with your understanding of your loved one. So hang in there as we go over the basics in part 1 and the specifics in part 2. It will have been worth it by part 3.

If you're a clinician, I hope this book gives you something to offer the family members of your OCD clients, and if you're an OCD sufferer, I hope it gives you a way to better articulate your experience to your loved ones. Most importantly, if you're a family member of someone with OCD, I hope it gives you, the *other one*, context for what's going on.

Part 1

Understanding OCD

There's a lot of information in these first three chapters. If this is the first book on OCD you've picked up, you may be relieved or disturbed by what you learn, so take your time, but don't insist on understanding everything before you turn each page. Trying to take in everything at once may be a bit overwhelming. You can always go back later. If, on the other hand, you've already done a lot of reading on the subject, then much of the following material will be review or may seem somewhat basic. Adjust your pace accordingly.

Chapter 1

How OCD Works and Where It Comes From

Given that you're reading this book, something possessed you to go online or go to a store and look for a book about someone else's disorder. Or perhaps your family member with OCD (or his therapist) suggested you read this book. Or maybe you were wading through books about OCD on some table at a mental health conference. *Are you at a conference right now for a disorder you don't even have?* (I'm right behind you...) How did this happen? Either you're lost or this is love.

Efforts to understand and help others are partly self-preservational. We need to defend our sense of self to keep other people's problems from tearing us apart. But it's mostly *love* that creates an intense urge to reach out and help. For most people, family trumps everything. Whatever may be going on in your personal life at any given moment, you would most likely drop it in a heartbeat for *family*. We want to relieve the suffering of our family members, because their suffering is simply unacceptable to us.

What OCD Feels Like

Having a mental disorder doesn't leave a tattoo on your face that identifies you as different from all the "normies," but there are certain characteristics and symptoms that identify the "sufferer" as a member of some kind of group. When I talk about "the OCD sufferer" in this book, I can't capture the experience of everyone with OCD, because no two people are alike—but I hope to represent what your family member is going through as best I can.

OCD is a disorder of internal discomfort, and whether they have OCD or not, everyone is afraid of something and finds certain things uncomfortable. Fear and anxiety are essential—if people didn't have these feelings in response to certain dangers, we all would have been eaten by lions long ago.

So take a moment right now to consider your own relationship to anxiety and fear. Consider for a moment just one thing or situation you consistently find uncomfortable or scary. For example, perhaps you're afraid of heights.

Now visualize being faced with your fear. If you're afraid of heights, imagine standing on the roof of a tall building. What would make your fear more troubling? For example, going with the fear of heights, imagine you're standing at the edge of the roof of this tall building, with your toes dangling over the rain gutter. Picture the street way down below, with tiny cars crawling along like ants. Imagine yourself closer to your fear than you've ever been.

Why does this situation or thing bother you? What exactly is it you fear will happen? Continuing with the heights example, consider that you might be off-balance—perhaps there's a gust of wind at your back. Consider that you might fall at any moment, and before you lies the terror of plummeting to the ground, followed by the pain of impact, followed by the uncertainties of death. Go ahead and be dramatic about it for a moment. Feel free to interchange it with different fears (the loss of a loved one, being diagnosed with an illness, being the victim of a violent crime, and so on). Put yourself right at the edge of your fear coming true. How would you feel? How would you know that you felt that way? Consider what your body would tell you. Would your heart be pounding furiously? Would your skin feel clammy or tight? How would your stomach feel in that moment?

You may feel a little "out of whack" right now in *this* moment. Maybe you started to feel some actual fear, even though you knew you weren't in any danger. Maybe you were able to briefly trick your mind and your body into believing that your fear trigger was present, that the consequences were real. It didn't matter that you knew it was all in your imagination. It still *felt*, just for a moment, like the real deal. Consider now that what you may have felt for that moment is what your family member with OCD feels on a regular basis—anywhere from one hour a day (the OCD diagnostic minimum) to not just every waking moment but also in his dreams.

OCD 101

OCD is the fourth most common psychiatric disorder (Pittenger et al. 2005) and the tenth leading cause of disability in the world (Murray and Lopez 1996). It's found in roughly 2 percent of the general population worldwide (Sasson et al. 1997). This percentage may vary based on age, onset, or other demographics across different studies, but generally, if there are a hundred people in a room, two or three of them probably meet the clinical criteria for a diagnosis of OCD. In brief, the *Diagnostic and Statistical Manual of Mental Disorders, Fifth Edition* (DSM-V) defines OCD as the presence of obsessions, compulsions, or both, which are time-consuming (more than an hour a day) and not better explained by any other condition (APA 2013).

Obsessions are unwanted intrusive thoughts. They're typically repetitive, disturbing, and ego-dystonic (meaning the thinker may feel that the thought poorly represents his identity). A person can have an unwanted thought about pretty much anything, but the types of thoughts most commonly problematic in OCD tend to fall into a few thematic categories, such as washing, checking, violent thoughts, and sexual themes. In the following chapter, I highlight a few categories that I've seen most frequently in my own practice.

Compulsions are physical or mental behaviors that can reduce the discomfort associated with obsessions. Just as all kinds of thoughts might become obsessions, pretty much anything a person can do has the potential to become a compulsion, so long as it's designed to relieve discomfort associated with an obsession. Some of the more common compulsions are excessive or ritualized washing or cleaning, avoidance of things that trigger the obsession, checking, seeking reassurance, mental review and analysis, and thought neutralization (trying to replace unwanted thoughts with wanted thoughts).

This back-and-forth between obsessions and compulsions creates a cycle, a loop of (1) experiencing discomfort from an unwanted thought, (2) attempting to reduce the discomfort, then (3) ultimately engaging in the very behavior that brings the discomfort back.

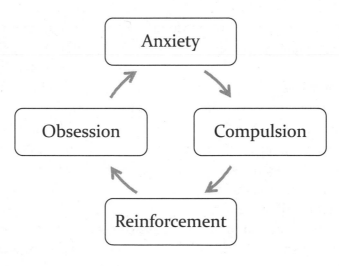

Figure 1

Let's say you become aware of an unwanted thought: *My hands might be dirty and I might get sick*. Uncertainty over whether this thought is just some random idea or a signal that something bad is about to happen, combined with a belief that dirty hands pose an imminent danger, causes you anxiety or disgust. To relieve this uncomfortable feeling and the sense that a problem has not been properly addressed, you wash your hands. Now, knowing that your hands have been recently washed, you feel more certain that they're clean. Because washing your hands resulted in relief from discomfort, your brain records this behavior (hand-washing) as something that should be repeated. This process is called *negative reinforcement*: the behavior is identified as a good one to repeat, because it removed (hence the word "negative") a painful experience. That means the next time you think *My hands might be dirty and I might get sick*, you'll have a stronger urge to wash your hands. As the connection between the two (the thought about having dirty hands and the action of washing your hands, which removes the discomfort) is consistently reinforced, your brain's demands for certainty about hand cleanliness go up, and it continues to increase the volume of its command: "Repeat! Repeat!" The intrusive thoughts about being dirty become more prevalent, more persistent, and more distorted as the compulsions become more complex and demanding and the associated pain of not knowing whether you're clean gets worse. To understand this concept as applied to other obsessions, consider that any thought, feeling, or physical sensation can be viewed as a "contaminant" or an intrusion on the mind, and a compulsion is an attempt to "cleanse" the mind of that intrusion.

The OCD Mind and the Spotlight Concept

Your family member with OCD actually has a spectacular mind. The way an OCD sufferer perceives the world is as if it has unlimited potential. Anything that can be thought of is possible, no matter how unlikely, and this is actually a *good* thing (sometimes). It fosters ingenuity, creativity, empathy, and a strong sense of humor. But it also comes with a burden, a painful awareness that everything is inherently uncertain and even the worst events imaginable are possible.

Maybe you yourself have a lot of negative "what if" thoughts too. A recent study demonstrated that nearly 94 percent of the general population across multiple cultures reports the presence of at least one intrusive thought. But OCD sufferers seem to find their thoughts more problematic (or more intense) and address them differently (Radomsky et al. 2014). They interpret unwanted thoughts as warning signals, as threats, instead of just random blips on their mental radar.

The unthinkable is indeed possible. Someone somewhere *has* died of a rare but terrible illness. Someone somewhere has lost her mind and committed an act of violence against a loved one. Someone somewhere has burned the house down by accident. *You* probably acknowledge that these things have happened but largely ignore them because the likelihood of them happening to you seems so low that the energy it would take to protect yourself from them is unnecessarily costly. As far as you know, the ceiling above your head could collapse at any given moment. You just don't think that particular risk warrants an investigation right now.

Your family member with OCD doesn't feel this way. Your family member struggles greatly to assess an appropriate response in cases where the risk is low but the potential loss is unbearably high. How far are you willing to go to protect a loved one from a tragic death? What if the thing you believed was protecting him was a ritual? What if that ritual consumed your life? Would you still do it, just in case? At what point would you really say, "I'm not willing to do *that* to keep my loved one from a tragic death?"

One way to conceptualize the difference between the OCD mind and the non-OCD mind is to look at what a mind really is. A mind, whether we discuss it as an organic part of the brain or as a more abstract or spiritual concept, is basically a tool we use to look at our thoughts and feelings. When someone says he's *thinking*, what he means is that he's looking at something that's going on inside his head and evaluating it. What he's looking with or *through* is the mind.

The Mindfulness Workbook for OCD (Hershfield and Corboy 2013) uses the concept of a spotlight to describe how the OCD mind works a little differently from the average mind. Picture your brain as a row of books on a shelf (figure 2). The mind is a spotlight that shines down on the shelf, illuminating the available information. The brightly lit information is quite obvious to you. The information at the edges of the light is obscured but still visible. The dark areas are where you go to dig up information on things you don't normally think about, whether positive or negative.

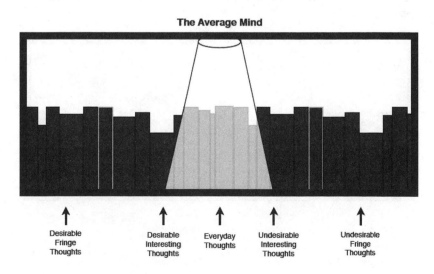

Figure 2

Now consider what it would be like if the spotlight of your mind was wider (figure 3), highlighting more of the available information. This wouldn't mean you were necessarily smarter, just more aware of the information on the fringe of most people's minds. On the positive side, it might help you come up with quick, clever ideas, an ability you've probably noticed in your family member with OCD.

On the negative side, the really scary unpleasant thoughts, the ones in the dark recesses of most people's minds, are as brightly lit as the mundane thoughts in the center of the spotlight. So instead of sounding like a quiet, muffled voice in the back of your mind, an idea like *What if there's a disease-causing germ on my hands?* seems a legitimate and important question, as relevant as "Do you see that the traffic light ahead is red and not green?" In other words, your family member with OCD notices fringe thoughts differently than you do. Though you and your family member may at times agree that these thoughts are silly or inconsequential, to your family member they're very much in the foreground. The bright lighting creates the illusion that these thoughts are intrinsically valuable, that merely *having* them is meaningful. This makes it seem terribly irresponsible to shrug them off or to make a simple remark to oneself like *That was weird* and move on.

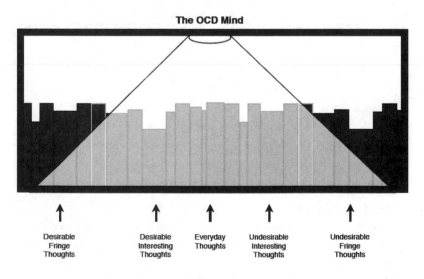

Figure 3

When a Family Member Has OCD

The issue is one of "How do I know for certain?" It may be easy for you to disregard a thought when it's quiet and obscured. But what if the same thought was loud and clear? How would you know it was safe to say "Oh well" and go back to living your life? This is the perpetual debate inside the mind of your family member with OCD.

Who Gets OCD and Why?

There are three main areas of interest when looking at the source of OCD: learned behavior, the brain (neurobiology and neurochemistry), and genetics. Research shows us that all three may play a role in developing and maintaining the disorder, but no single one guarantees someone will have it.

Family Environment

In terms of learned behavior, we might consider the role of a person's upbringing in how she learned to cope with uncertainty and other areas that are difficult for OCD sufferers. When looking at the research, it's important to remember that when two issues coincide, it doesn't necessarily mean that one issue causes the other. For example, Timpano et al. (2010) found that children whose parents were authoritarian—rigid, rule-oriented, and not very nurturing—were more likely to have OCD symptoms and related beliefs than children whose parents were permissive or authoritative. Some research also suggests that paternal overprotection and an overly interfering rearing attitude may contribute to the development of OCD (Yoshida et al. 2005). This doesn't mean that children raised in authoritarian or overprotective households will necessarily develop OCD or that those raised under different conditions won't. Furthermore, it's unclear whether authoritarian parenting contributes to the development of OCD or is a strategy for addressing the presence of OCD.

Another area of interest in upbringing and OCD is the role of *expressed emotion* (EE), a measure of emotions and attitudes involved in communication between family members. High EE is characterized by emotional overinvolvement (being overly emotional, demonstrating extreme self-sacrifice and making it known), criticism (making negative comments), and hostility. These qualities overall are associated with higher rates of OCD in families (Przeworski et al. 2012).

There's a chicken-and-egg conundrum here. In other words, OCD affects family functioning, which affects OCD, especially in the way in which family members respond to an OCD sufferer's symptoms and behaviors (Renshaw, Steketee, and Chambless 2005). The members of an OCD family simply interact with one another differently from the non-OCD family. Parents whose children have OCD may be less likely to engage in constructive problem solving, less encouraging of their child's independence, and less confident overall in their child's abilities (Barrett, Shortt, and Healy 2002). Are you nodding your head in agreement, or are you thinking *This sounds nothing like my family?* Either response is perfectly normal. Further exploration is needed to provide families with the best treatment tools. Though little empirical evidence supports the idea that the family itself directly causes OCD, there remains some kind of reciprocal relationship in which symptoms affect and are affected by the family system (Waters and Barrett 2000).

The Brain

Research suggests that there are certain differences in the brains of OCD sufferers compared to the brains of people without OCD. OCD seems to be related to decreased gray matter (fewer cells and nerve fibers that make up brain tissue) in the medial frontal gyrus, the medial orbitofrontal cortex, and the left insulo-opercular region, as well as increased gray matter in the putamen and the anterior cerebellum (Pujol et al. 2004). OCD patients also show structural differences in the cortical and thalamic regions (Rotge et al. 2009). If all this terminology gives you a headache, suffice it to say that people with OCD have more gray matter in some areas of the brain and less in others, as well as more activity in some areas of the brain and less in others.

One way of understanding OCD and the way it can result in a seemingly endless loop of worries and worried responses is by looking at the functions of different areas of the brain and how a mistake in one area can have a domino effect.

The area of the brain known as the *thalamus* is partly respon-sible for storing information about the body. The thalamus sends information to the *caudate nucleus* and *basal ganglia*, which are areas associated with memory, learning, emotion, and several other functions. In a way, this is where the important messages are filtered from the brain's equivalent of junk mail. If this filtering system incorrectly identifies a piece of junk mail as an important notice, it can trigger a false alarm in the *amygdala*, which is the area responsible for identifying threats. The amygdala alerts the *orbitofrontal cortex*, the front part of the brain where we do all of our calculations and analysis. This part of the brain tends to be hyperactive in people with OCD, so the problem is compounded (Beucke et al. 2013): the message about the threat not only is a false alarm, but is being overly processed as legitimate. This analy-sis, essentially validating that the alarm is *not* false, gets kicked back to the parts of the brain responsible for preparing us for danger.

Picture the brain sending signals to the body to prepare for battle. Heart rate goes up, breathing becomes more rapid, muscles tighten, and so on. This bodily experience is recorded by and pre-sented again to the part of the brain where the filtering takes place. Now we have something going on physiologically suggesting that something actually *is* wrong. The message is approved by the filter and sent to the front part of the brain for more hyperanalysis. It all began with one little glitch, but now brain and body are stuck in a loop of feeling as if something's wrong, thinking something's wrong, and strategizing to make things right.

People with OCD tend to have abnormalities with respect to specific *neurotransmitters* (chemical messengers in the brain), most commonly serotonin, glutamate, and dopamine. Medications used to treat OCD typically help regulate these neurotransmitters by increasing or decreasing their presence or availability in the brain. (See chapter 3 for more on how OCD is treated with medication.)

Genetics

Your family member with OCD may be the only person with OCD you've ever met. But if you look at the big picture and the patterns of behavior that have been studied across families, there's no doubt: OCD tends to run in families.

Here are a few things we know from research:

- The risk of OCD is significantly increased when a first-degree relative has OCD, or a related disorder such as generalized anxiety disorder, body dysmorphic disorder, social anxiety disorder, or panic disorder (Steinhausen et al. 2013).

- A child whose parent has OCD is more likely to have some kind of social, emotional, or behavioral disorder similar to OCD (Black et al. 2003).

- There's a higher-than-average prevalence rate for OCD in immediate relatives of people with OCD (Nestadt et al. 2000).

Exactly which genes play a part in OCD is still unknown. As of this writing, a collaborative genetics study may have identified a genetic marker associated with learning and memory as being related to OCD (Mattheisen et al. 2015). However, several genetic studies suggest that multiple genes, each influencing a person's predisposition toward developing OCD, are at play (Taylor 2013). The hope is that one day we'll understand the relationship between genes and OCD so that we can tailor medical and therapeutic treatments to what's happening in the brain of the OCD sufferer.

Are You to Blame for Your Family Member's OCD?

You may think it's your fault—that you *gave* your family member OCD somehow. Sure, if it's your kid, you may figure it's your genetics, but a genetic predisposition to OCD has many different implications—some good, some bad. It's not your fault if raising your children by setting boundaries you thought were reasonable caused your children anxiety. It's not your fault if your husband with OCD can't accept your reassurances and keeps demanding more and more answers in hopes of relieving his pain. You didn't cause that pain. OCD caused that pain. It's not your fault if your little sister can't give you a hug because she associates it with painful thoughts of having done something terrible. She has a different brain than you do and is doing the best she can with it. She loves you the way she can—for now. Maybe she'll be able to express her love with a hug one day.

If you fear that you may have caused your family member's OCD, I want you to free yourself of any blame you believe you deserve. Feelings of guilt won't help you in your effort to support your family member with OCD. Considering that OCD is largely about intolerance of uncertainty, challenge yourself in this moment to accept that the mechanisms behind your loved one's OCD are complex. Ultimately, having OCD is no one person's or concept's fault. It certainly isn't the OCD sufferer's fault, yet you'll find your family member with OCD carries a fair amount of guilt about having it. When she sees the pain she's causing your family, it's easy for her to forget that she's not totally to blame. She is, after all, doing the behaviors that are causing the pain. How can she not see herself as at fault? Well, she has a mental health issue that drives her to do those things. It wedges her between painfully distorted thoughts and pointlessly impairing behaviors. She wants desperately to leave the obsession behind, to put an end to the rituals, but the pain of doing so seems too great. The good news is that, although the causes of OCD aren't clear yet, research continues to open up more efficient paths to better treatment.

Is There a Cure?

OCD is considered a chronic condition (Rasmussen and Eisen 1997), and it waxes and wanes throughout life. The word "cure" implies the disappearance of all symptoms. Since experiencing painful unwanted thoughts is a symptom of OCD, "curing" the disorder would entail eradicating all unwanted thoughts. Yet unwanted thoughts are a completely normal part of the human experience; having no unwanted thoughts would actually be a sign of a different sort of problem with the brain. By the same token, rituals are symptomatic of OCD, but they're also part of the normal human experience—they relieve us of the responsibility of having to think about everything we do while we're doing it, and they provide a measure of comfort and predictability.

So we have to have *some* unwanted thoughts, and we have to have *some* rituals. But do we have to be slaves to these unwanted thoughts and these rituals? Do they have to impair our functioning, reduce our quality of life, isolate us from our families and society? No. With appropriate treatment, the "D" in OCD—the disorder—can be reduced to background noise, to something we can simply comment on with "Well, that's just how I think sometimes. I don't need to do anything about it right now."

So when the word "cure" comes up in the context of OCD, it's misleading for all involved. OCD can't be cured, because it's not a disease. It's a lot of things—genetics, learned behavior, and personality, to name a few. What we should be aiming for is not a cure for a disease but mastery of a disorder. Unlike other conditions labeled "chronic," OCD is one in which a person, with the right tools, can expect to get better and better over time.

Consider This

If you know a bit about the things your family member with OCD obsesses about, take a moment to consider the lengths to which he goes to complete his rituals and why he believes the hope of ridding himself of certain thoughts and feelings is worth it. What would you have to think or feel in order to justify putting that much effort into getting it to stop? What would you have to believe to make the choice to continue despite knowing your loved ones want you to stop?

Your Struggle

You just finished the first chapter of a book that you're reading for someone else's benefit. Whether you're directly involved in accommodating your family member's rituals, or whether you're just a silent observer wishing you could do something to help, you're spending a huge amount of energy on someone other than yourself. Consider how your reasons for doing so relate to your values. Where do those values come from, and how do they help you persevere? Take a moment to notice the internal contradictions inherent in your journey to understand your family member's OCD: It may bring you pain to enter this new world of obsessions and compulsions your family member experiences, but then at the same time you may notice feelings of relief, anticipation, or even joy knowing that new tools and new hope are on the horizon.

Chapter 2

Common
Manifestations of OCD

As much as you fear that your family member's OCD will impair her life, she fears it too, but she also fears that you'll fail to understand her OCD. Your family member already feels as if something is wrong with her, but the more insight she has into her disorder, the more she feels like a sane person trapped in a crazy person's body. Among the more painful aspects of the disorder is the thought that you, her loved one, see the "crazy" part more than the sane part trapped inside. Her biggest fear is that you'll come to the conclusion that what you *see* is what she is.

Below you'll find an explanation of a few common manifestations of OCD I've seen in clinical practice. Some people's obsessions fall into a single category, but many people struggle with a potpourri of obsessions. This doesn't necessarily mean their OCD is worse, only that their obsessions have a wider range of content. Maybe your family member struggles with a fear that doesn't fit into any of these categories. Again, this has no bearing on the severity of his disorder or the legitimacy of the obsession. If you don't see the theme of your family member's OCD below, you might find it described in one of the books listed in the resources.

We give these obsessions names mostly because those who suffer from OCD use these names to help reduce their pain of isolation. A person who has intrusive thoughts of a violent nature may say, "I have Harm OCD." Harm OCD is not a *kind* of OCD as much as a theme of the unwanted thoughts. Being able to say to another OCD sufferer, "Oh, you have Harm OCD too?" helps alleviate the shame associated with having these thoughts. Still, it's important to remember that this doesn't mean one kind of OCD is fundamentally different from another, because they all involve obsessions and compulsions.

Contamination Obsessions

One of the most common obsessions is an excessive concern over cleanliness, hygiene, and fear of items in the environment that are considered "contaminating" (Rasmussen and Eisen 1992). OCD sufferers without contamination obsessions often find the popular emphasis on the subject to be somewhat irritating (OCD isn't all about hand-washing!), and those who suffer with it may often find themselves dismissed as "neat freaks" or germophobes. In reality, if your family member struggles with Contamination OCD, he feels as though he's under constant attack from objects in his physical environment. These might include germs, which many people worry about, but also dirt, bodily fluids, chemicals, insects, intoxicants (for recovering alcohol and drug addicts with OCD), dust, hair, *schmutz*, or any substance a person might come in contact with that triggers an urge to wash or clean it away.

If your family member has Contamination OCD, she lives in a world covered in wet paint. It feels as if everything she touches is "getting on" her, and thus she's spreading contaminants to whatever she touches next. On the surface, it may appear that she's just "clean" or demanding, but the reality is she spends most of her time feeling filthy, as if she's drenched in toxins, trying to reduce this sensation by more and more washing. The washing itself becomes such a burden that she washes even more just to preempt even more washing after that. This can even lead to avoidance of washing, because the effort it takes to feel clean is so extreme she'd rather not try. But then, in a perpetual state of contamination, she can't function either.

For some, the sense of being contaminated involves unwanted thoughts about getting sick or about getting others sick. For others, being "contaminated" has more to do with bad luck and the idea that if they engage in activities while contaminated (including the activity of thinking about things!), then those activities themselves may become contaminated with bad luck. For others still, their contamination obsessions are driven by a fear that the feeling of disgust about being contaminated would be overwhelming (Cisler et al. 2010). And for others, obsessive concern with contamination comes from a fear that *less* concern with cleanliness might mean they were socially irresponsible.

If your family member has Contamination OCD, you may wonder how he can be so particular about some things and so complacent about others. How can he wash his hands 100 times a day yet leave garbage on his bedroom floor? There are two explanations for this behavior. One is that OCD is inconsistent. Rules are created in the mind, but so are loopholes in those rules, and if the OCD sufferer feels as though he has permission from the OCD to do something, even if it's something that seems relevant to his obsession, the feeling of being "allowed" prevails. (Sometimes in treatment it's necessary to focus on breaking "OCD rules" for this reason.) The other explanation is that your family member feels as if he can't touch certain things. This creates a paradoxical world in which he must always remain clean, but he can't come in contact with things that need to be cleaned. So his hands get washed, but dirty laundry gets left on the floor and avoided.

Don't judge yourself too harshly if you think this is somewhat ridiculous. It boggles your mind and it doesn't make sense because you can't help but look at it from a more logical standpoint. That's how *your* mind works. Just try to remember that your family member may be operating with different equipment up there. Two people can be fully aware that HIV isn't an environmental contaminant and can't be spread by shaking hands with strangers, for example. But the person who knows this and feels contaminated after a handshake has to make a choice to consciously assume a risk that the feeling is a false alarm. That takes effort on her part, and it can be exhausting. Though it may look as though your family member is making things up on the spot when her OCD rules are inconsistent, it's unlikely she's creating those rules just to manipulate you. More accurately, she's the one being manipulated by OCD.

Things you might observe your family member with contamination obsessions doing:

- Spending excessive time in the bathroom, at the sink, or in the shower:

  - Washing; rinsing; drying

  - Wiping after using the toilet

  - Cleaning areas of the bathroom after use

- Laundering excessively

- Avoiding showering or other washing/grooming (because ritualized washing/grooming is too daunting a task)

- Using soap or toilet paper excessively

- Using hand sanitizer excessively

- Repeatedly getting up to wash during meals or other activities

- Avoiding public restrooms, railings, crosswalk buttons, remotes, or other commonly touched items

- Avoiding tasks associated with cleanliness (dishes, laundry, and so on)

- Refusing to use/touch clean objects (video game controller, computer, clean laundry, and so on) after being "contaminated"

- Reacting emotionally to "contaminated" objects

- Asking repeated questions about how to wash, what's clean, what's safe to touch, what was touched, or whether something was washed (including whether she had washed)

- Confessing that various items may have been touched or hands may not have been washed enough

- Demanding accommodations (that you wash or avoid things, open doors for him, and so on)

Other things your family member with contamination obsessions might be doing (things you won't observe):

- Reviewing (or retracing) what she has touched and whether she has touched other things subsequently (for example, *My hand touched my dirty car keys, which I put on the counter, which is next to the fruit bowl, where I got this orange, which means my clean hands now touching this orange may be dirty from my keys, which have touched my pocket, which I had put my hand in after touching the car door handle...*)

- Mentally neutralizing—rationalizing why his hands are clean (for example, telling himself over and over that there's no documented case of anyone getting cancer from a doorknob)

- Scanning the environment for contamination threats (for example, mold on the wall or someone touching their nose)

- Comparing herself to others to determine whether her hand-washing is sufficient (often with the belief that her own hand-washing should be more thorough and more "responsible" than another's)

- Tracking *your* behavior to make sure *you* haven't become contaminated

- Spending hours internally debating whether he's contaminated enough to wash or clean enough to not wash

Your family member with contamination obsessions might be concerned that:

- You'll get hurt in some way because of her failure to decontaminate or complete her rituals sufficiently.

  - If the washing is a ritual to neutralize a "bad thought," then failing to wash could result in any number of terrible events, including you getting hurt or killed in a way unrelated to contamination.

  - If the washing ritual is germ-focused, then failing to wash could result in her getting sick or getting something on her that transfers to you and gets you sick. Then you might die (or at least resent her for not being vigilant enough and for ruining your life). If a stranger gets sick and dies because of her failure to perfectly complete compulsions, then she may be a murderer and you may reject her accordingly.

- You'll think he's irresponsible, filthy, or disgusting for failing to wash or clean something that you would've washed or cleaned. This is often a pervasive concern because his OCD tells him that his standard for washing must be higher than any standard he's aware of, just to ensure that it's not lower than any possible standard that could exist.

- You'll think she doesn't love you when she chooses rituals over participating in family interactions.

- You'll stop loving her when her OCD becomes unbearable to be around.

- You'll stop loving her if treatment doesn't work (often leading to treatment avoidance and self-sabotage).

- You'll suddenly stop accommodating his compulsions, and he'll feel contaminated forever. (How to stop accommodating in a gradual and healthy way is covered in part 2.)

You might be concerned that:

- Repeated washing strips the skin of protective oils and healthy bacteria, resulting in damaged skin, prone to infection.

- Excessive use of soap, water, and so on poses a financial burden to your family member and to the family as a whole.

- Your family member's demands for accommodation are expanding, and you may not be able to keep up. You're trying to help, but it doesn't seem to be working; however, you worry that if you suddenly stop, she may fall apart.

- Your family member is missing out on important family interactions, events, special moments, and so on.

- Your family member's compulsions are impairing her functioning to an extent that she can't seem to take care of herself, hold down a job, balance her finances, engage in basic hygiene, and so on. You worry how she'll ever get by without your help.

- Conflict between you and your family member over his OCD is eroding the relationship. It's all about the OCD, and the two of you—your personalities, your inside jokes, the connection you once shared—seem to be fading away.

Hyper-responsibility (Checking) Obsessions

Your family member with OCD doesn't want the house to burn down, doesn't want the car to get stolen, doesn't want there to be a home invasion. Sounds reasonable, right? Except he *really* doesn't want those things to happen. More than *you* even, and you *really* don't want them to happen. His fear isn't just that these unwanted things will occur, but that he'll discover he was responsible for them somehow. He may think: *"If only he had checked to make sure the door was locked," they'll say. "If only he had checked the light switch, then the electrical shortage that caused the spark that burned down his family's home could have been prevented!"*

Hyper-responsibility OCD puts the sufferer in the pilot seat of a plane carrying precious cargo, every single second of the day. It's okay if you think this is just dramatic—that's how it looks from the outside. Maybe, when the two of you leave the house, you think your family member is just being annoying when she has to go back inside to make sure a light bulb is securely screwed in. It's okay to have those feelings. Actually, for many OCD sufferers, that's how it looks from the inside too. The thing to remember is that your family member who's launching a full-scale investigation of the doorknob for the tenth time is trying to get a feeling to go away. Her brain is dumping chemicals into her body that hurt. They hurt as if the house has been broken into and it's all her fault. If she checks the lock, the hurt goes away. She walks back to the car, where you're furiously clutching the steering wheel, trying not to flip out on her for making you late (again), but as she starts to put on her seat belt—there it is again, that feeling.

"Just let it go!" you want to scream at her. *She ruins everything!* you think as you look at the clock and realize you're going to be late for one more thing because of her OCD. She knows it too. Further, she very likely knows what a burden she has been. That's a different kind of pain, though. That's about sadness. Sadness is no walk in the park, but it's not as powerful as the terror of what she thinks might happen if she doesn't give in to her compulsive urges.

When *you* close a door, turn off an appliance, or put something back where you found it, something clicks in your brain that says "Good enough. Task completed." It's a subtle but convincing feeling that allows you to move on to the next task. Imagine if you got the *opposite* feeling after doing those things. If you were staring at a locked door, thinking about how you just locked it, but *feeling* as though the task wasn't completed, what might you do? You'd very likely check the door, or unlock it and lock it again, trying to get that feeling. Maybe it would work. Then you'd walk away. What if it didn't work? Well, you'd probably try again and maybe add something to it, something like saying out loud, "Hey, I'm locking the door, see?" Maybe that would work. What if it didn't? Before you know it, you might be trapped in an endless cycle of repeated rituals. In the OCD brain, this cycle is self-perpetuating. The part of the brain responsible for saying "Good enough. Let's move on" isn't doing its job. The rituals replace this (at least a little), making that part of the brain grow lazy, even less efficient than before, making the sufferer more dependent on checking.

Hyper-responsibility OCD can involve significantly more than just checking to make sure something is off or locked. It also has to do with a heightened sense of moral obligation to take fringe thoughts as seriously as humanly possible. For example, imagine seeing a pebble in the street. It would probably be of no interest at all. The street is made of pebbles, and some of them are loose. Now consider what it would be like if noticing the pebble triggered a movie to start playing in your head. In the movie, a car drives over the pebble, and the pebble goes flying. Cut to a small child playing innocently in his front yard, running around with a toy airplane, looking up at the plane, imagining being a great pilot one day. Cut to a slow-motion close-up of the pebble flying through the air, in a line drive for the boy's head—it's too late. The boy is hit in the eye. He's blinded by the impact. His horrified family rushes him to the emergency room. He survives, thank goodness, but he never becomes a pilot. His life is ruined. He drowns in depression and alcohol. *If only you'd checked more closely and removed the pebble from the street instead of selfishly minding your own business!* Would you take just a second out of your day to check for pebbles?

Things you might observe your family member with hyper-responsibility (checking) obsessions doing:

- Checking locks, stoves, doors, light switches—anything electrical, anything that opens or closes

- Excessively checking e-mail and social media (This may be hard to distinguish from simply browsing or wasting time online.)

- Repeatedly opening and shutting things to make sure they're appropriately opened or shut

- Returning to see whether anything bad might have happened while she was away, such as coming home from work in the middle of the day to make sure the garage door was really closed or circling around to make sure the speed bump she drove over was not in fact a hit-and-run victim

- Taking unusual risks to ensure that nobody gets hurt by accident (for example, climbing down a subway platform to remove a coin from the tracks for fear the train might derail)

- Investigating and/or picking up random items that might possibly be dangerous if left behind

- Asking questions or seeking reassurance about checked items to get confirmation—that the lights have been turned off, the stove is not on, and so on (or demanding that *you* check)

When a Family Member Has OCD

- Performing secondary rituals associated with checking to feel more certain the task is being completed, such as tapping, saying certain words, or counting

Other things your family member with hyper-responsibility (checking) obsessions might be doing (things you won't observe):

- Devoting mental energy to constructing an image of the checked item (for example, picturing the door locked)

- Retracing the steps of a checking ritual to feel certain that the ritual was appropriately completed

- Researching statistics regarding tragic mistakes (for example, the likelihood that a house would burn down if a stove was left on or the likelihood of being burglarized because a door was unlocked)

- Silently counting or performing other mental rituals while checking, in order to feel certain that the checking is being done correctly

- Mentally reviewing and rationalizing why it's okay or not okay that he checked or didn't check something

- Reviewing and dwelling on constant pervasive feelings of guilt that she hasn't been responsible enough (This may be accompanied by self-punishing thoughts, berating herself for not being certain enough that her fears won't come true.)

Your family member with hyper-responsibility (checking) obsessions might be concerned that:

- You'll get hurt as a consequence of his failure to appropriately check.

- You'll resent her or blame her for losses associated with her failure to check (for example, your home was burglarized because she left the door unlocked, your possessions burned because she left the stove on).

- You'll think of him as irresponsible or a criminal (for example, because he believes he may have hit someone with his car and didn't go back to see whether anyone was hurt).

- You'll think she's selfish or uninterested in your priorities (such as your desire to leave the house to get to the airport on time) when in fact she's terrified to leave without completing her checking rituals.

You might be concerned that:

- Your family member is suffering professional, academic, or social impairment (for example, repeatedly being late for work or other important scheduled activities due to checking rituals).

- Your family member is irritated much of the time due to her hyper-responsibility burden, and this makes you feel as though you have to walk on eggshells around her, trying not to get into a fight.

- Your family member is missing out on important family interactions, events, and special moments because she's "in her head" obsessing about something to be checked instead of enjoying life.

- Your family member's checking rituals may get worse and may continue to disrupt family functioning.

Just Right Obsessions

Just Right obsessions have to do with an overwhelming urge to make sure that things appear or are done in a very particular way.

When a Family Member Has OCD

This can manifest as a need for things to be symmetrical or organized in a specific way. It can also manifest as a form of perfectionism, needing something to look a certain way or feel a certain way. You may not see a method to the madness, but your family member with OCD knows exactly what she's looking for by how she feels when she sees it.

Your family member with OCD isn't "picky." He more likely feels that if he doesn't have things one way or another, the discomfort of *knowing* that will annihilate him. It may seem altogether goofy that a person needs to line things up "just so" or touch something on the left side only because it had been touched on the right. But imagine what it would feel like to know you had one untied shoe. Now imagine that you're on a long and beautiful nature walk and you can see the untied lace bouncing around, hitting the ground, hitting your ankle. Maybe you even trip over it. You think, *All I have to do is stop walking, kneel down, tie the shoe, and get on with my life.* But everyone says not to worry about it. Everyone says your shoe is fine the way it is. They say that you're being annoying, that you should just let it go, or that it's not important. You start contemplating what the rest of this long walk will be like if you can't tie your shoe. You won't enjoy the fresh air, the exercise, or the scenery. All you'll be able to think about is your discomfort with the untied shoe. It will be torture knowing that enjoyment of the walk is just out of reach, with that nagging shoelace taunting you the whole time. By now you'd rather abandon the walk altogether if you can't tie your shoe.

Now consider that the long walk is a metaphor for life in general. What if life just didn't feel right enough? What if life was mostly about chasing a feeling that always seemed just out of reach? What if you could get a taste of that feeling by doing something—just once, then again, then another time, as much as it took for you to feel just right?

Also common in Just Right OCD is *magical thinking*, in which the sufferer is concerned that failure to get things "just right" might have far-reaching consequences. Let's say it occurred to you that failure to line items up symmetrically on your desk might somehow cause your mother to get diagnosed with a terminal illness. You might think, *Oh, that's a silly thought*, but what if it coincided with a twinge of guilt and an increase in your heart rate? How easy would it be for you to resist the urge to fix something, *just in case*? How would you feel if you believed you might have taken a risk with your mother's life because you didn't make something small just right?

Things you might observe your family member with Just Right obsessions doing:

- Lining up items in a specific way (not necessarily symmetrical, sometimes intentionally asymmetrical)

- Frequently "fixing" things to make them the way they're "supposed to be"

- Repeatedly touching or tapping items (often to complete some ritual associated with them having been touched)

- Repeating routine tasks (going in and out of doorways, turning light switches on and off, et cetera, until the right feeling is achieved)

- Needing to perfectly understand what he reads, or needing to have each letter of the alphabet he writes look a certain way

- Asking you to fix things for him or to repeat things until he understands them perfectly

Other things your family member with Just Right obsessions might be doing (things you won't observe):

- Perpetually analyzing whether things feel right or not

- Experiencing pervasive guilt over not having fixed things adequately

- Mentally reviewing whether it was okay to leave something the way it was

- Thought neutralization (trying to make things "just right" with thoughts)

- Mentally replaying events, things he did, or things he said until they feel right

Your family member with Just Right obsessions might be concerned that:

- You'll think she's "anal" or perfectionistic, arrogant, or snooty because it looks as though she has to have it "her way."

- He's responsible for how his day, or your day (or life), may go from here on out depending on whether his rituals have been completed.

- You'll get annoyed with her, think she's stupid, or find her irritating.

You might be concerned that:

- Your family member can't seem to relax or enjoy himself.

- Your family member will get hung up on some small detail and "ruin the moment."

- Your family member will get angry if you don't allow him to ritualize.

- Your family member's rituals are making you or other family members late for scheduled events.

Sexual Obsessions

Sex, sexuality, sexual orientation, and sexual concepts overall carry a mix of profoundly personal feelings and perpetual uncertainty. Sexual thoughts and feelings are a petri dish for OCD and may involve unwanted thoughts about sexual orientation, incest, or pedophilia and fears about engaging in sexually aggressive or deviant behavior (Williams and Farris 2011).

If your family member has OCD with sexual obsessions, it doesn't mean he's a pervert, having a sexual orientation crisis, or simply weird. He just has a "what if" locked in his vault, and he's struggling to break it out. You might not "see" a lot of the compulsions associated with sexual obsessions, because many of them are covert. You might notice that your family member avoids certain things that may trigger unwanted sexual thoughts (some of these things may be more predictable than others), or you might be on the receiving end of a lot of compulsive confession of or reassurance-seeking about unwanted sexual thoughts.

Sexual obsessions can be a particularly lonely form of OCD in which the content of the unwanted thoughts is so taboo the sufferer dares not reveal it to anyone, even close family members. This isn't necessarily because of a lack of trust; it's a reflection of the high level of shame associated with the obsessions. As with other obsessions, the actual thought content, however unpleasant to the thinker, is bound to be the sort of thing that may have popped into your own head from time to time. The difference is the sense of urgency of addressing these what-if questions.

You may come across the term HOCD or SO-OCD to describe obsessions about being or becoming a different sexual orientation or POCD to describe obsessions about being or becoming a pedophile. It's important to remember that these abbreviations have no clinical meaning and are simply part of the lexicon of the OCD community. OCD is a disorder of obsessions and compulsions; the content of the obsessions doesn't matter to the diagnosis. In other words, there's nothing especially peculiar about people with sexual obsessions.

If your family member struggles with sexual obsessions, however, he likely thinks he's defective for having them. He's consumed by a simple fear that something is wrong with him sexually.

Though it may be a trend in psychological circles to theorize about what this means in secret, what it means in reality is that your family member is normal—simply terrified of not being so. This is probably the most important thing you can remember as a family member of someone with sexual obsessions. It's not about the content of the thoughts. There isn't something to explore, there's no threat of him acting out, and he doesn't have a sexual problem. He has dysfunctional strategies for dealing with unwanted thoughts. He responds to sexual what-ifs with attempts to prove, convince himself, or guarantee that his fears are unreal, and because of this, his fears become more impairing.

A lot of what you'll hear in the more proving-focused obsessions (especially sexual obsessions and violent obsessions) is "I know I'd never do this or be this kind of person, but I have to be sure." The problem with this is that the more you try to prove something that you already believe to be true, the more doubt you'll experience. Try it for yourself: Take a look at something you're wearing, and notice what color it is. What color is it? Do you know that for sure? Of course, if you can see color, you can see what color your clothing is. Now, imagine you felt a responsibility to be *more* certain about what color your clothes were. What you could do was tell yourself "My clothing is the color _____" every few minutes for the rest of the day. So every five or so minutes, just ask yourself what color your clothing is and then tell yourself that it's that color. A funny thing happens when you do this. What you thought was blue starts to feel as though it might be a hue of gray or turquoise. This is because your brain constantly strives to explain your behavior, and the only reasonable explanation for repeatedly telling yourself the same thing is that you must be missing something. This leads to doubt, which leads to more efforts to convince yourself. Now consider that if your family member has OCD with sexual obsessions, she's doing pretty much the same thing, only trying to get certainty that she's not a sexual deviant, a danger to children, a sexual threat to a sibling, or of the "wrong" orientation. At the core of sexual obsessions is often the fear of being in denial. The sufferer imagines the shame involved in one day having to "admit" her fears are more than just OCD. It's torture, and, without treatment, the drive to keep doing compulsions grows infinitely.

Things you might observe your family member with sexual obsessions doing:

- Expressing excessive disgust regarding triggering material (for example, homosexual love scenes in films)

- Avoiding environmental triggers (for example, not wanting to be near a school for fear of sexual thoughts about children)

- Avoiding sexual intimacy

- Avoiding any tasks that might trigger unwanted thoughts (for example, changing a child's diaper)

- Confessing and seeking reassurance about sexual thoughts, including repeatedly asking whether such thoughts make him whatever he's afraid of

- Refusing to discuss anything sexual

- Researching sex and sexuality, on the Internet in particular, in hopes of finding reassurance that her fears are unfounded

- Repeating behaviors, such as body movements, or reenacting his behaviors to reassure himself that he wasn't doing something inappropriate

Other things your family member with sexual obsessions might be doing (things you won't observe):

- Reviewing every thought for potential sexual content

- Testing to see whether he's attracted to certain people (including checking for groinal sensations in certain situations)

- Deeply analyzing hypothetical sexual events (for example, *If given the opportunity, would I have engaged in this sexual act?*)

- Reviewing every past sexual act for evidence of deviance

- Seeking reassurance by looking at pornography and researching sexuality

- Punishing herself and experiencing self-hatred, pervasive shame, and guilt for having thoughts she finds unacceptable

- Analyzing things *you* do or say to determine whether they're indicators that you believe there's something wrong with him sexually

Your family member with sexual obsessions might be concerned that:

- You'll think she's a freak, a sicko, or a fool.

- You won't believe he has OCD and will abandon him.

- She'll find out she doesn't have OCD, and you'll hate her for misleading you.

- You'll think he's a danger to children or capable of committing a sexual crime.

You might be concerned that:

- Your family member (your partner) has stopped enjoying sexual activity.

- Your family member is never free, never enjoying the moment, because he's always thinking.

- Your family member is missing out on social activities in her attempt to avoid triggers.

- Your family member is missing out on being a parent, dating, or other opportunities because of his fear.

- Your family member doesn't appear to trust you or your ability to understand what she's going through.

- There's some other psychological issue at hand that isn't being addressed.

Violent Obsessions (Harm OCD)

Have you ever been driving and felt a sudden urge to steer into oncoming traffic? Have you ever stood next to someone at a bus stop and wondered what was stopping you from just shoving that person into the street? Have you ever been trying to get your kids to go to bed and right before you're about to leave, one of them asks for one more thing and you feel so enraged your whole body tenses up as if you're about to punch someone? Have you ever been watching a news story about a crime of passion (for example, a jealous lover who stabbed her partner) and thought for a moment you might be likely to do the same thing? Have you ever found yourself threatening to murder telemarketing "robots" if they call you again? (Come on, I can't be the only one who has.)

Harm OCD takes these normal but sinister thoughts and presents them as warnings. This suggests to the thinker that he could have, would have, might, can, or is capable of committing an act of violence—perhaps an act of violence against a loved one, an act of violence against a stranger, or an act of violence toward himself. As with sexual obsessions, there may not be a lot of noticeable rituals other than avoiding triggers and seeking reassurance that the fear is unreasonable. For most Harm OCD sufferers, the struggle is mostly internal, and they're not particularly keen on talking about it with anyone.

Obsessive thoughts of violence are like rapid-fire intrusions of vivid violent imagery, horrified feelings, and intense physical symptoms of anxiety. It's as if there's a TV inside your head that's stuck on the horror movie channel, and the only button that works is "Volume UP." Imagine, just for a moment, you're sitting down to dinner with your family. You're about to cut into a delicious steak, and you reach for the knife. When your hand makes contact with the handle, suddenly a scene tears through your mind, like a flashback in a movie. You see yourself clutch the knife, then plunge the blade into the person sitting to your left. He screams, cries, yells in anger, then begs to understand as he dies in front of you. Chaos ensues; the police arrive; you can't explain why you did what you did. Everybody hates you. You're tried, convicted, and sentenced to death. Then you snap back to reality, but you don't feel much like eating anymore.

The question at the heart of Harm OCD is *What if I hurt someone?* Because in life some people really do hurt one another, the question seems legitimate at first. Much as with sexual obsessions, if your family member has Harm OCD he's on a quest to eradicate any shred of suspicion that any harm could possibly come to anyone he's responsible for (including himself). Harm OCD may focus on "snapping" or going mad, making the sufferer fear public places where he might go on a rampage. More commonly, however, it targets the people the sufferer cares most about: spouses, siblings, children, or parents. Self-harm obsessions can manifest as well, in which the sufferer fears committing impulsive or unpredictable suicidal acts. This is different from actually *being* suicidal. The sufferer fears somehow losing control and *becoming* suicidal. Whatever the fear, doing compulsions makes the feared outcome seem less likely in the short term. That's why rituals are so compelling: they offer a temporary sense of relief and safety.

If your family member has violent obsessions, that doesn't mean he's a closeted Hannibal Lecter. To the contrary, it means he's so offended, so profoundly disgusted by the same violent thoughts everybody has from time to time that he'll do anything to get rid of them. The problem is, that entails doing rituals, and rituals make the thoughts louder, more intrusive, and more distorted.

Things you might observe your family member with violent obsessions doing:

- Avoiding knives, scary movies, anger in general, or anything she associates with unwanted violent thoughts

- Avoiding people she thinks she might harm

- Avoiding situations where acting out a violent thought feels more possible (going on a camping trip, staying home alone with the children, and so on)

- Asking lots of questions about the difference between someone with OCD and a sociopath (this often includes a lot of online research into the subject)

- Confessing unwanted violent thoughts

- Asking for confirmation that he'd never harm anyone

- Performing secondary rituals aimed at neutralizing bad thoughts, such as tapping, repeating, or counting

- Demanding that triggering items (for example, knives) be kept out of sight

Other things your family member with violent obsessions might be doing (things you won't observe):

- Mentally reviewing and analyzing all intrusive thoughts, combing through them for evidence of danger

- Thought neutralizing—actively trying to replace unwanted thoughts with positive ones (for example, mentally repeating the word "save" to try to cover up the intrusive word "kill")

- Retracing and reviewing experiences for evidence of harm or the potential to cause harm

When a Family Member Has OCD

- Experiencing constant and pervasive guilt over having violent thoughts in the first place

- Analyzing your behavior and things you say, to get certainty that you don't think she's a harm risk

Your family member with violent obsessions might be concerned that:

- Despite doing all his rituals, he may miss one and you'll get hurt, or find him having hurt himself.

- You'll think she doesn't really have OCD and is just crazy or dangerous, and you'll call the police or have her admitted to a mental institution.

- You're not safe around him.

- You'll decide she's horrible.

You might be concerned that:

- Your family member isn't participating in family life.

- Your family member causes a scene at times because something triggered her OCD.

- Your family member doesn't love you or want to be near you.

- Your family member will start convincing herself of her obsession and act out in a dangerous way (particularly with self-harm obsessions).

Religious Obsessions (Religious Scrupulosity)

Does your family member with OCD pray all the time? He may be someone of great faith, truly connected to his higher power. But what happens to some people with OCD who are religious is that their faith becomes the focus of obsessive thoughts. After all, OCD tends to target whatever the sufferer cares about the most. For a religious person, her connection to her higher power may very well be the most cherished of connections. If you think about how compulsions reinforce themselves by relieving the pain of unwanted thoughts, as discussed in chapter 1, consider how powerful the urge must be to relieve the pain of unwanted thoughts about God.

If your family member has religious obsessions, he may be burdened with intrusive thoughts of blasphemy or doubts about his beliefs. Just like other obsessions, religious obsessions don't have much to do with what a person actually believes. They have to do with what he *fears*. So he sets out to prove them wrong. But when connecting to his faith becomes a nightmare, prayer becomes just another ritual and the threat of losing his connection with his higher power becomes a self-fulfilling prophecy. He tries to think only the "right" thoughts and ends up falling short. Then the "wrong" thoughts come pouring in. These might be thoughts about behavior considered sinful (sex, violence, and so on), thoughts about not believing enough or in the right way, or uncertainty about understanding or following religious scripture perfectly. Sometimes religious scrupulosity is just about technicalities. If your religion teaches you to pray a certain number of times a day, how can you know for sure that every time you prayed counted as actual prayer? What if one time it wasn't a "real" prayer and you were just going through the motions? *Better do it again, just in case.*

And then there's the afterlife. Someone with OCD whose religious beliefs include eternal reward or punishment may be burdened with intrusive thoughts about that punishment and may be doing compulsions in hopes that it will prevent her worst nightmare. If your family member suffers from religious scrupulosity, the nightmare is self-perpetuating. *If I don't do this, I'll go to hell. But doing this makes me feel as if I'm already there.* It's a double bind, because whereas religious faith demands acceptance without proof, OCD demands proof before acceptance. If your family

When a Family Member Has OCD

member hands over the responsibility of sorting out the details to his higher power, that might be good, but how does he know exacly which details to hand over? If your family member obeys his compulsive urges and tries to get certainty about his religious obsession, he isn't really practicing faith, and what might the consequences of that be?

Things you might observe your family member with religious obsessions doing:

- Praying excessively; repeating prayers; performing prayers in overly rigid ways

- *Avoiding* places of worship, for fear that unwanted thoughts will appear or fear that the rituals necessary for getting through it are too daunting (Recall washing avoidance in Contamination OCD.)

- Reading religious materials excessively, for compulsive prayer or for reassurance

- Confessing to and seeking reassurance from family members and religious advisers

- Miscellaneous rituals that may be associated with warding off blasphemous thoughts (for example, repeatedly walking through a doorway, rewashing her hands, or chanting certain words)

Other things your family member with religious obsessions might be doing (things you won't observe):

- Silently praying and attempting to control or block thoughts that conflict with her religious beliefs

- Analyzing the meaning of specific religious scripture and whether it applies specifically to her

- Mentally replaying discussions with spiritual advisers, in an attempt to reassure herself about a religious concept

- Repeating self-reassuring statements, such as *God will forgive me if I make a mistake, God knows I'm trying my best*

- Compulsively punishing herself (for example, forcing herself to repent or engage in some other act to pay for potentially sinful behavior)

Your family member with religious obsessions might be concerned that:

- You think he has lost faith.

- You resent her for being rigid or difficult.

- His failure to perform rituals will have consequences to you (for example, he's praying to keep you from harm).

You might be concerned that:

- Family practice of faith is no longer happening or is no longer pleasant.

- Your loved one appears to be in a state of constant suffering.

- Your loved one has become judgmental or critical of the way *you* practice *your* faith.

Moral Obsessions (Moral Scrupulosity)

Similar to religious scrupulosity, moral scrupulosity is an obsession with doing or having done the exact right thing in accordance with certain beliefs, only here in an exclusively nonreligious or moral context. Moral obsessions can cover a wide range of topics. They may be focused on seemingly insignificant actions, such as never putting an aluminum can in the trash rather than the recycling bin; or they may have to do with big ideas, such as never being unfaithful to one's partner.

The morally scrupulous worship at the altar of "good person," but their mind is always telling them that they're not cutting it. They often appear brutally, painfully honest, to the point of absurdity, because of their pervasive fear of being dishonest. They can't see the forest for the trees, focusing on the details of what they said, what they felt, and what they intended at each given moment, all in the service of trying to get certainty that they're good and righteous people.

Right now *you* are doing something immoral…sort of. You're not attuned to it unless you have morally scrupulous OCD. But if you're reading this book in print, you may be holding a little piece of rainforest violently chopped away from a little piece of some marginalized indigenous people who depend on the forest for their survival. If you're reading this as an e-book, your ability to do so comes from the power of the microchip, made of a metal mined in possibly the most horrifying work conditions imaginable. You're still a good person from where I'm standing, and I'm sorry to bring these details to your attention. But imagine what it must be like for your family member, for whom such details are always in the spotlight and for whom "letting it go" feels like not caring about humanity, the worst of all possible crimes.

Moral scrupulosity can also manifest as a battle with intrusive "bad" thoughts. The thoughts might be racist, sexual, crude, or vulgar—anything the sufferer finds unacceptable to say out loud. It's as if the presence of such a thought is the same as shouting it from the rooftops, and the sufferer's conscience won't be clear until his mind is cleansed. The key thing to remember about your family member, if he suffers from moral scrupulosity, is that he's likely consumed by guilt at any given moment. Whether he recognizes that the guilt is nonsensical, it still hurts like a knife, and compulsions seem like the only relief.

Things you might observe your family member with moral obsessions doing:

- Confessing unnecessary details of events

- Putting on excessive displays of morality (for example, making sure people can see his wedding ring so that they know he has no intention of cheating)

- Apologizing excessively for real or imagined events (or for having bad thoughts)

- Seeking reassurance regarding right and wrong or about the meaning of past events (this may also include demands that you confirm his morality verbally)

- Avoiding moral "gray areas" (for example, by boycotting various products, stores, or activities)

- Excessively checking to ensure she didn't cheat or break a rule (for example, repeatedly going over tax forms)

- Doing rituals associated with morality (for example, washing a second time because it would be insensitive to allow any germs to transfer to another person)

- Being honest to a fault (for example, actually answering the question "Honey, does this make me look fat?")

Other things your family member with moral obsessions might be doing (things you won't observe):

- Experiencing pervasive, unyielding guilt and self-hatred

- Mentally reviewing past events that triggered obsessive thoughts

- Analyzing alternate versions of past events (for example, *What would I have done if...?*) or potential future events (for example, *Would I do the moral thing if...?*)

When a Family Member Has OCD

- Punishing himself; criticizing himself; repeatedly telling himself that he's bad or not good enough

- Thought neutralizing—replacing immoral thoughts with supposedly moral ones

Your family member with moral obsessions might be concerned that:

- You'll think she's bad. (Your opinion as her family member may be the only one she believes, making you the one whose reassurance she seeks most often.)

- You'll find out that he's bad and abandon him.

- She's hurting you by being dishonest about how bad she "really" is.

You might be concerned that:

- Nothing seems to make your family member feel good enough about himself.

- Your family member isn't mentally present or "tuned in" for family activities.

- Your family member has changed, has become too serious, or can't have fun.

- Your family member's confessions will harm your relationship (for example, if your partner repeatedly confesses attractions to other people).

Relationship Obsessions

"Really." The word "really" is the key word in relationship obsessions. The question sometimes starts with a simple, unassuming thought: *What if I don't love my partner?* It's meaningless, non-threatening, and random. *Of course I love my partner.* But what if I don't *really* love my partner? That's a different question; that's a question about certainty. Once the question becomes about certainty, your loved one with OCD feels a moral obligation to attempt to prove the unprovable. It usually begins with some form of emotional checking, trying to see whether he *feels* love, and from there it spirals out of control.

On the surface, it looks like doubt about the relationship. If you're the partner, it looks like doubt about you. (*Doubt About You* would make a great sitcom title.) More accurately, it's doubt about herself. Your family member is stuck on the fact that she has an unwanted thought about you. It could be a thought she believes is true but is attaching way too much importance to. It could also be a thought she doesn't even believe in the first place! It could be a thought about an element of your appearance, your belief system, your past, or anything else. The thing is, she loves you so ridiculously much that unwanted thoughts about you seem too threatening to brush off. It's the terrible thought of losing you that makes the compulsions seem so necessary. In other words, your family member loves you more than she can handle. Weird compliment, sure, but embrace it.

If you're in a relationship, picture your partner. Consider something about this person that makes you uncomfortable. It could be something small, like the fact that he takes unusually large bites of food. Now imagine you had the kind of mind that took these facts and somehow bound them tightly to your love. Imagine that every time you felt love for your partner, you'd be presented with a loud, bright image of him chewing an oversized piece of food (or doing whatever else makes you uncomfortable). What if it just stuck that way, and for the rest of your life you had to smile at your partner while hiding your disgust over the unwanted image in your head? For people with OCD, unwanted images and ideas become stains. They become something you can't help but think about, even if you know they're irrational and even if you'd rather think of anything else. What would you do to save the relationship? Whatever it took to get the images and ideas unstuck, probably. For your family member, that means doing rituals, and they make it worse.

Things you might observe your family member with relationship obsessions doing:

- Confessing significant relationship fears or doubts

- Excessively seeking reassurance about the health of the relationship (including researching books and articles on relationships)

- Asking excessive questions about your past and your feelings about it

- Excessively saying "I love you" and other reassurance-inviting statements

- Avoiding intimacy in an attempt to avoid worried thoughts about the health of the relationship

- Engaging in excessive intimacy as an attempt to get reassurance that the relationship is healthy

- Avoiding behaviors suggestive of a healthy future (meeting your parents, taking a vacation together, and so on)

- Falling into a sudden sour mood when something triggers his OCD (at times including anger at you for unwittingly engaging in the triggering behavior)

Other things your family member with relationship obsessions might be doing (things you won't observe):

- Constantly analyzing the relationship

- Feeling that she's in denial or lying about her love for you

- Feeling a desperate desire yet inability to connect to the present moment

- Deeply analyzing all things related to relationships

- Deeply analyzing everything you say, to determine whether it means something about the relationship

Your family member with relationship obsessions might be concerned that:

- You'll give up on her.

- He doesn't deserve you.

- She'll destroy your life by having "led you on" and then changing her mind.

- You'll think he's just jealous or controlling; you won't believe his behavior is OCD.

You might be concerned that:

- Your family member actually has serious doubts about the relationship.

- You're not good enough for your family member.

- Your family member is being selfish or mean, and she's not the person you thought she was.

Consider This

If you read through each section above, you spent a lot of time analyzing, studying, and, well, judging your loved one. This is not a crime. This is the only way a person without OCD can understand a person with OCD. But take a moment to consider what that might feel like if you were the one with OCD. People with OCD get read about, they get evaluated, they get prescribed this and that, and most of them do it because they'll do anything to get better. But it hurts. It hurts to be an "other" and to be studied and looked at and wondered about. Consider what it must be like to wish you could blend in.

Your Struggle

So far, you probably read a lot of things that are heart-breaking, maybe disturbing—certainly confusing. You might have read a lot of things that weren't really relevant to your family member's specific challenges with OCD. (Since it's possible to obsess about anything, it's impossible for me to cover every obsession out there.) You've put up with a lot of your family member's symptoms at home, and now you're putting up with this book's attempt to cover the basics of understanding a family member with OCD. You do this because you care. You care because this person is family.

Chapter 3

Diagnosis and Treatment

If your family member has already been diagnosed with OCD, perhaps the diagnosis came as a relief, or perhaps you worried about your family member being "mentally ill." Diagnosis is an important part of the healing process. These days, a lot of people who are just picky or particular say things like "I am so OCD about _____," which misrepresent the severity of impairment and disruption in family life that occurs with real OCD. Some people criticize the use of diagnoses in helping people overcome challenges because of a belief that we shouldn't categorize people or have them self-identify as sick. I disagree with this on a number of levels, and as an OCD sufferer, having a name for the way I think is a game-changer. It reminds me that when I get overwhelmed by unwanted thoughts and feelings, it isn't some failure of character or some ugly personality trait. It's a clinical condition, and there are clinical tools to help me develop mastery over it. Having a diagnosis means I'm not doomed or completely alone in the universe; instead, I share a specific set of characteristics with millions of people around the world. It benefits me to this day to remember I have an OCD diagnosis, even if at times I find myself thinking I should hold out for an eleventh opinion.

What a Diagnosis Looks Like

Ideally, a diagnosis should occur after an assessment by a psychiatrist, a psychologist, or any mental health professional who has been trained to assess for mental illnesses. The most common way of assessing OCD is with the Y-BOCS, the Yale-Brown Obsessive Compulsive Scale, a list of over fifty common obsessions and compulsions (Goodman et al. 1989). It may come in the form of a rating scale to determine the severity of symptoms or a basic checklist of obsessions and compulsions. Childhood OCD is most commonly assessed with a version of the Y-BOCS called the CY-BOCS (McKay et al. 2003). In addition to the use of an assessment tool like the Y-BOCS, an initial meeting with a clinical professional will likely include a clinical interview, including questions about the history and impact of the symptoms. (See chapter 11 for the different types of treatment providers and how to access them.)

A mental health professional may also use family-based assessment scales to better understand the role that OCD plays in your family. The OCD Family Functioning (OFF) Scale can be used to assess the level of impairment in the family system caused by OCD, including the emotional impact (Stewart et al. 2011). The Family Accommodation Scale (FAS) can be used to assess the ways in which family members accommodate the OCD (Calvocoressi et al. 1999).

Not everyone can afford or access a qualified professional to receive a diagnostic assessment, but that doesn't prevent a person with OCD from working on getting well. I'd encourage anyone who suspects they have OCD to read some of the better-known books on OCD (see the resources) and the information provided on the website of the International OCD Foundation (http://www.iocdf.org). Avoid putting much stock in online self-tests for OCD.

If your family member can access a qualified professional but is hesitant to get diagnosed, try to find out what the roadblocks are. For example, he may be afraid of being labeled, he may feel ashamed to have family money spent on his illness, or he may be afraid of being told he has something more upsetting than OCD. Later in this book, I discuss why reassurance is often unhelpful, but this is one area where reassurance is perfectly acceptable. Emphasize that a diagnosis doesn't define a person but unlocks the toolboxes for getting better. Empathize with his fear of opening up to a stranger, of telling the whole gruesome story to someone he just met. And above all, let him know you'll be there to support him the whole way.

Understanding Your Role in Treatment

You don't have to be an expert in OCD treatment to be an expert in helping your family member with OCD. In fact, putting yourself in the position of "expert" may be counterproductive. The golden rule for supporting a family member with OCD is to remain a family member. You're not her therapist, and it's unlikely to benefit her if you try to be. Your family member with OCD actually relies on family support more than you might think. Though her struggle with OCD is an inwardly lonely journey—even others with OCD can't understand *exactly* what it's like for her—it shouldn't be an outwardly lonely one. Your family member with OCD should see family and home as a place to come back to after therapy and feel close to her loved ones. If you act as though you're her therapist, it will create distance between you. Then she may feel alone both inside and out. So be a mom, be a dad, be a brother, be a sister, be a son or daughter to your loved one with OCD.

This doesn't mean you're forbidden from adopting therapeutic qualities. Like a therapist, you may treat your family member with a form of unconditional love and kindness, and you may be his advocate. And you may be his cheerleader, pointing out when he's headed in the right direction and when he appears to have derailed. But you're not responsible for his treatment, you're not the definitive source of professional psychotherapy, and you're not bound by the same legal or ethical constructs as a therapist. This is a good thing. No non-professional relationship could withstand this amount of pressure.

All this being said, as a nonexpert, you need to know enough about OCD and its treatment to have some tools for supporting your loved one and for coping with your own struggle. What follows is a basic overview of what any family member would benefit from knowing about OCD treatment.

The Basics of OCD Treatment

If your family member is getting competent treatment for OCD, he'll typically be getting something called *cognitive behavioral therapy* (CBT), medication, or some combination of the two. The use of CBT and medication is typically well tolerated and produces meaningful symptom reduction (March et al. 1997).

Cognitive Behavioral Therapy

Cognitive behavioral therapy (CBT) is often referred to as the "gold standard" of OCD treatment. A recent meta-analysis (study of multiple studies) found that CBT consistently produced better results than relaxation exercises, anxiety management training, pill placebo, and other control conditions (Olatunji et al. 2013). CBT involves three core elements: psychoeducation, cognitive therapy, and behavioral therapy.

Psychoeducation

When a therapist provides psychoeducation to a client, he's literally teaching the client about OCD. The first part of a relationship between a CBT therapist and a client is a teacher-student relationship. The OCD sufferer is the one who really has to do the work to get better, so she has to start by learning what she's up against and what she'll be doing to master her disorder. So therapy for OCD starts with a know-your-enemy approach. In time, this teacher-student relationship will become more of a coach-athlete relationship, in which the therapist teaches, guides, and promotes the therapeutic tools and principles.

Cognitive Therapy

The term *cognitive* refers to cognition, or thinking. Your family member with OCD is burdened by the presence of unwanted thoughts. But it's not the *presence* of these thoughts that's the problem. We all have pretty much the same kinds of thoughts; we just respond to them differently. It's the way in which someone with OCD experiences and appraises these thoughts that makes them seem more urgent, more threatening. So the drive to get rid of them with rituals is far greater. In cognitive therapy for OCD, the OCD sufferer is asked to identify how his assessment of a situation might be distorted and what it might look like if he could reframe his thinking to something more objective. It's not so much about challenging the rationality of the obsession—like my arguing with my little one over why the color of the lid of her milk bottle on any given day isn't that important—but challenging the *need* to respond to the obsession with a compulsion.

These skewed thinking processes are called *cognitive distortions*. Here are a few examples. For a more comprehensive list of cognitive distortions common in OCD, see *The Mindfulness Workbook for OCD* (Hershfield and Corboy 2013).

All-or-nothing thinking is when you believe that things are either all one way or all the other way. For example:

- *My hands are either clean or dirty.*

- *I'm either straight or gay.*

- *I'm either a good person or a bad person.*

- *I'm either connected to my faith or I have no faith.*

- *I'm either in love with my partner or we're incompatible.*

This type of thinking makes it really hard to resist compulsions and really easy to get bullied by the OCD. For example, at this moment I consider my hands clean. I washed them shortly before sitting down to write this. However, it's doubtful that this computer keyboard is clean. So, technically, my fingers probably have germs on them. If I get stuck thinking of my hands as being either totally clean or totally dirty, the drive to wash and rewash can be unbearable. If I say they're clean, then anything they touch makes them dirty and I have to wash. If I say they're dirty, then I have to wash. In the end, so that I can write instead of wash, I have to override an obsession with the cleanliness of my hands by accepting that they're just *hands* and are somewhere between clean and dirty.

As the supportive family member, try to challenge your own all-or-nothing thinking. Your family member with OCD needs you to see her as a full person. If you perceive her as either "sick" or "well," then you'll become burdened by a need to constantly fix her "sickness" or preserve her wellness. Then the relationship will become about her being "sick" or "well" instead of about *her*.

Catastrophizing is when you predict a negative future and assume you can't cope with it. You may hear your family member with OCD saying things like "If _____ is true, I'll die," or "The plane is going to crash," or "If I don't wash, I'll get sick." Catastrophic thinking pervades all forms of OCD, but the key element is the belief that the feared outcome is too much to risk because it would be impossible to cope with. In the end, we're incapable of predicting the future; recognizing this allows us to say "I don't know what will happen." This is a stronger position for resisting compulsions than saying "I have to make sure the bad thing doesn't happen."

You're understandably worried about your family member. That's why you got this book. But quite often we get so caught up in ideas like "If he doesn't get better, life will be unbearable" that we start doing things that make it worse. Consider how accepting that you don't know the future for your family member but will surely find a way to deal with it will help you focus on supporting him.

Disqualifying the positive is when you disregard evidence that runs counter to the obsession. You may have noticed that the reassurance you've offered to your family member doesn't seem to last. This is because of the emphasis the OCD places on *this time*. "Sure, I've never hit anyone with my car and failed to notice it before, but *this time* I may have, and I need to go back." "Sure, my doctor says the mole looks normal, but *this time* he didn't examine it as thoroughly and seemed to be in a rush to get me out of his office." People with OCD tend to embrace ideas that support their fears and push aside evidence that refutes them. This may seem totally irrational, but from the perspective of someone with OCD, it's a safety issue. To your family member, it may feel unsafe to assume that things will work out. It may feel as if the responsible thing to do is take all threats (even imaginary threats) seriously.

It may have crossed your mind that you aren't very good at supporting your family member with OCD. Because after all the effort you've put in—reading books like this one, taking him to his appointments, accommodating his needs or trying not to accommodate his needs, whatever his therapist says you're supposed to do—he's still suffering. You see your family member engage in a ritual, and suddenly all the work you've put into being supportive seems forgotten. Your biggest fear is that he'll never be happy or healthy, and when you see him engaging in unhappy, unhealthy behavior, you forget all the progress he has made (and perhaps your role in it). That's also disqualifying the positive.

Tunnel vision is when you overfocus on things related to the obsessive thoughts. This is essentially the inverse of disqualifying the positive, because it involves "letting in" only information that supports the obsession. For example: You and your family member with Contamination OCD walk into a restaurant. Whereas *you* notice that the food smells nice and the music sets a pleasant mood, your family member notices only the stains on the menu, covered in disease-causing bacteria. Perhaps you're nodding your head right now, thinking, *Everywhere we go, that's all she sees!* You're quite right. Her OCD brings to her attention the items in her environment connected to the obsession, keeping her from seeing outside the tunnel. If she works on recognizing that she has tunnel vision and that noticing something doesn't make it more important, it will help her resist the compulsive response.

You also have OCD on the brain, just not necessarily *your* OCD. Because you have a family member who's struggling with OCD, you hear about OCD, talk about OCD, think about OCD, and deal with OCD on a pretty regular basis. Your world becomes OCD. You too can fall victim to tunnel vision if you become too attuned to your family member's symptoms. You may start to see OCD in all of your family member's behaviors, even those that are just quirks or unrelated to the disorder. You may start missing the big picture of your family member and latch on to every hand-wash, question, or repetition he engages in. That puts you too often in the role of warden or accuser, creating conflict and distance between you and your loved one. He has OCD, but he's not *just* his OCD.

Emotional reasoning is when you believe something is true because it *feels* true. You've probably seen your family member seemingly frozen in time, completely stuck on an idea. You want to tell him, "Just let it go; move on; drop it." But you don't feel the way he does about whatever it is he's stuck on. Because it *feels* dangerous or wrong to move on, it must *be* dangerous or wrong to move on. Would you walk away from a baby if you thought it was in harm's way? What if your gut told you that the baby was in harm's way, but your spouse told you otherwise? You might "know" that your spouse was right, but it sure wouldn't *feel* that way! Being able to recognize that we can feel one way and act another is hugely important for an OCD sufferer. It takes tremendous strength to go against our feelings. Normally they can be trusted, but when it comes to OCD, it's as if there's something in the brain pressing down on a *feeling* button (guilt, terror, regret, you name it). The outside world says not to trust it, that it's just OCD, but the inner world paints a different picture.

You may feel guilty about refusing to participate in one of your family member's compulsions. You may think that this guilty feeling is evidence of having done something wrong. And yet, any book on OCD (or any OCD therapist) will tell you not to give in to your family member's OCD. So this means you may have to sit with this guilty feeling but not *reason* that it means you're doing the wrong thing. Instead you'll have to look at the big picture: recognize that you're doing what needs to be done to help your family member overcome his OCD and that this feeling is just an unfortunate by-product.

Overestimating responsibility is when you believe that you alone are responsible for keeping bad things from happening. This is when your family member feels profoundly and personally responsible for any tragic events that might occur due to her being less vigilant than her OCD demands. Her OCD may demand that she wash to keep others from getting sick, prove her sexual orientation to keep her marriage safe, pick up a piece of tree bark to make sure no one uses it to stab someone—the list is endless. Being able to recognize that responsibility has limitations and that OCD is demanding an infinite amount of responsibility may make the difference between choosing to tolerate discomfort and running into traffic to compulsively remove a thumbtack.

We feel responsible for the health and happiness of our family members. It's a basic part of being a family. And it's not just that parents feel responsible for their kids. A teenage boy can feel responsible for his big sister, and a grown woman can feel responsible for her father. We can't help it, and that's a good thing. But when you want something so badly, the way an OCD sufferer wants certainty about his obsessions, you start to think that you must take on full responsibility for things working out. When you inevitably fail to achieve this impossible demand, it leads to burnout and resentment. Being a truly supportive family member means handing over a little, a lot of, or practically *all* responsibility to your loved one for getting a handle on his OCD. Letting go of responsibility is no easy feat, but it's often the only thing that works. For an OCD sufferer to overcome his symptoms, he has to choose to resist compulsions. Without the element of choice, his brain will never recalculate the appropriate response to unwanted thoughts.

Behavioral Therapy

As a strategy for helping people change the way they think and feel, behavioral therapy focuses on modifying what people *do*. The form of behavioral therapy most commonly used in CBT for OCD is known as *exposure with response prevention* (ERP), and it's extremely effective at reducing OCD symptoms (Franklin et al. 2000). In fact, if your family member is in treatment for OCD but isn't doing some form of ERP, then he's probably not getting the appropriate help. (Note that some forms of CBT, such as acceptance and commitment therapy, may not use ERP specifically but nonetheless are effective because they employ techniques that encourage nonavoidance of fears.)

I tried explaining to my six-year-old what I do for a living. It went something like this: "I talk to people about what they're afraid of and then we go and try to find it. Once we catch it, I teach them how to deal with being afraid until it stops seeming so scary." I think she thinks I'm some sort of wizard, but that's pretty much what an OCD specialist does. *Exposure* is about bringing the feared thought or situation closer. Once you have it right in front of you, you can practice responding to it differently. By differently, I mean without compulsions—hence *response prevention*. Once the brain witnesses the feared situation without the compulsive response, it has to recalculate its position that the feared situation always warrants a compulsive response. If the situation doesn't demand washing, or cleaning, or avoiding, or reassuring, then it must be somehow capable of being accepted even if it remains uncertain. Once acceptance of uncertainty begins to set in, anxiety (which is the brain's way of telling you to flee danger) diminishes, because it becomes a waste of resources.

At the core of behavioral therapy is the concept that we all have control over our behavioral choices. This may be hard to accept at first. Compulsive urges are overwhelmingly powerful and feel impossible to resist. "I can't just stop" is something you've likely heard your family member with OCD say many times. But the truth is there's more to that statement: "I can't just stop *without horrible pain*." By working with an OCD specialist, your family member can learn to stop doing compulsions gradually and learn healthy strategies for coping with the pain.

When we change our behavior, changes in our thoughts and feelings follow, because one thing the brain can't stand is our thoughts, our feelings, and our behaviors being inconsistent with one another. If you behave a certain way long enough, your thoughts and feelings will fall in line with whatever that behavior demonstrates. This is true for doing compulsions, which demonstrates fear. It's also true for doing exposures, which demonstrates confidence.

ERP typically starts with creating a hierarchy of feared situations, a list of exposure challenges from easiest to hardest. Though some people learn to swim by being thrown into the deep end of the pool, most people learn better gradually, by mastering one step at a time. Overcoming an obsession is much like learning to play a musical instrument: first you learn how to hold the instrument, then you learn to play scales, then you learn to play simple songs, then you learn to play more complex songs, and then you learn to write your own songs. Giving someone a musical instrument and pushing him out onto the stage just creates more fear.

Once the therapist and the OCD sufferer have drawn up a framework establishing which exposures will be attempted and when, the therapist supports and guides the OCD sufferer through ERP exercises. In most cases, ERP exercises are performed during the therapy session and then assigned as homework for practice between sessions. *In vivo* exposures involve making contact with fears in real life. For example, someone who's afraid of germs may practice exposure by touching the therapist's desk and then practice response prevention by delaying or resisting washing her hands. Once she can tolerate that, she moves up to something more challenging for her, like touching a public railing. *Imaginal* exposures are used to confront hypothetical or abstract obsessive fears and usually involve writing exercises in which the sufferer imagines his fears coming true. The response prevention element there involves resisting the urge to neutralize or self-reassure.

As your loved one continues to gradually expose herself to her fears and practice response prevention, her perspective will shift and her anxiety will generally begin to decrease. This process of fear reduction, called *habituation*, is traditionally the primary purpose of exposure. Recent research suggests that what may be occurring in the brain is something called *inhibitory learning*, in which repeated exposure to a feared situation teaches the person that the situation is not only potentially dangerous (excitatory) but also potentially safe (inhibitory) (Craske et al. 2008). This more accepting, nonthreatening perspective of the situation competes in the brain against the less accepting, fear-based perspective. This happens whether the anxiety stays or goes, so learning to accept and tolerate anxiety is as important as (maybe more important than) learning to reduce it. So in the end, even though your family member's anxiety very likely will go down after repeated exposure, he'll learn that he can still function *with* anxiety and *without* engaging in compulsions.

Building strong brain muscles. The best way to build muscle is by lifting heavy weights. But you can't start with the heaviest weights or you'll hurt yourself. And you can't have someone lift the weights for you either (as my trainer pointed out). Doing repetitions at the appropriate weight necessarily involves discomfort, but over time it results in being stronger. You can imagine there's a brain muscle responsible for tolerating uncertainty. ERP exercises strengthen that muscle in your family member by having her lift mental weights.

For you, too, there are brain muscles to strengthen and fears to overcome. Watching a family member with Contamination OCD struggle because he feels contaminated and is trying to resist washing is painful. You may feel a powerful urge to give him the hand sanitizer, knowing that this is a compulsion (for both of you!). Watching a family member squirm with anguish because she wants to ask you the same reassuring question just one more time and knowing all you have to do to ease her pain is give in is something you have to gradually build a tolerance for if you're going to help her get better. As you learn to reduce your behaviors that accommodate your loved one's OCD, you'll have to learn to tolerate increasingly painful feelings associated with her pain. But if you overcome your fear of crumbling under the pressure of her suffering, she'll be free to overcome her obsessions.

Mindfulness

When I was a kid, there was this pretty red bird, a cardinal, that would crash into the living room window around the same time pretty much every day. He'd crash hard (*bonk!*), shake his head, and fly off. Then he'd come back at around the same time the next day and fly right into the window again. One day, my mother decided to open the window and, lo and behold, the cardinal flew into the house. She opened a window on the other side, and he flew out after a short while. We never saw him again. I don't know why he was so determined, but he was going to go *through* our house, not above or around it. Your thoughts and feelings are very much like that cardinal, whether you have OCD or not. They must go *through* you. Pain is a product of resistance, so the more a thought or feeling seems to be tearing you apart, the more likely it is that you're getting in the way. The noise in your head is the sound of thoughts colliding with locked windows. Mindfulness is like opening your windows and allowing those thoughts through, even if you'd prefer they stay outside. It's the best form of giving up.

Mindfulness is the concept of paying attention to the present moment without judgment. In the case of OCD, it means allowing yourself to observe your thoughts, feelings, and physical sensations as being only what they *are*, not getting caught up in what they could mean. A thought about the stove being on becomes exactly that—a thought—the content of which has to do with the stove. A thought about the stove being on is not a mandate to check the stove to make sure it's off. A feeling of impending doom, something your family member with OCD may experience often, is not a *sign* of impending doom. It's a feeling. A tingling sensation in your arm is exactly that, not necessarily a warning that you're having a heart attack. To use mindfulness to combat OCD is to openly acknowledge upsetting thoughts and related urges to do compulsions, but to more or less sit in the audience and watch them taking place on the stage. This may involve learning to meditate and practicing mindfulness from one moment to the next with the help of various exercises. Mindfulness can significantly enhance the effectiveness of CBT for OCD (Fairfax 2008).

Consider that when you're watching your family member struggle with a compulsion, you probably feel an urge to comfort him, advise him, or avoid him, any of which can help you get rid of an uncomfortable thought or feeling. A mindfulness approach would ask that you take a moment to simply observe that thought or feeling, and observe that desire to do something about it, then choose your response. Sometimes no response at all will be the most helpful response for you and your family in that moment. But not responding when someone you love is seeking relief from anxiety or engaging in a disruptive behavior will take willingness on your part to stay uncomfortable too.

Medication

The decision to take medication for OCD is a profoundly personal one, but medication often plays an important role in treatment. Unless your family member is too young to make her own decisions on the matter, keep your personal opinions about medication to yourself. This isn't meant to sound harsh. It's just that if you're against medication, remember that *you're* not the one being persecuted by the unwanted thoughts and anxiety; your family member may welcome the relief that medication can bring. If on the other hand you're for medication—maybe you take similar medication yourself—remember that medications come with risks and potential side effects, and they can affect people differently. In the end, your family member (if of age, and with the consultation of a psychiatric professional) must make the decision.

The first-line medications for OCD are a class of drugs called *selective serotonin reuptake inhibitors* (SSRIs) and also a tricyclic antidepressant called clomipramine (Kellner 2010). Research suggests that OCD symptoms largely have to do with serotonin (a neurotransmitter, or chemical messenger in the brain), which is understood in part due to the anti-obsessional effects of serotonin reuptake inhibitors (Greenberg, Altemus, and Murphy 1997).

Common SSRIs are fluoxetine (Prozac), fluvoxamine (Luvox), sertraline (Zoloft), citalopram (Celexa), escitalopram (Lexapro), and paroxetine (Paxil). For a good primer on medication for OCD, see "Medications for OCD" at http://www.iocdf.org/about-ocd/treatment/meds.

Dosage

The American Psychiatric Association recommends higher doses of SSRIs for the treatment of OCD than for depression and other disorders (APA 2007). SSRIs are typically effective for OCD when taken in the highest doses allowed. This can involve a long, slow process of gradually increasing the dosage until your family member has arrived at a dose that works for her. Higher doses of SSRIs are correlated with a greater reduction in OCD symptoms than lower doses (Bloch et al. 2010). Your family member should speak to the prescribing doctor about the therapeutic dose of the particular medication he's considering and the pace at which he'll work up to that dose.

Side Effects

The most typical side effects of medication for OCD are sleepiness or, alternatively, insomnia; constipation or, alternatively, diarrhea; and sexual side effects. Sexual side effects can be particularly frustrating (especially if your family member already has sexually themed obsessions). To support your family member, let him know you support his bravery in taking medication. Never suggest that going on medication is the "lazy" route. It isn't. Plus, OCD has a way of chipping away at the sufferer's self-esteem and self-worth, so that many OCD sufferers just don't think they deserve relief from their pain. Others think they're cursed and just hope not too many people will abandon them. When they reach a place where they're willing to put chemicals in their body with unpredictable results, they're often thinking, *I just can't keep doing this to my loved ones. Whatever it takes, I must get better.* Don't discourage that.

When medications for OCD work, they can transform lives. They seem to do this by accomplishing a few important things:

- Decreasing the intensity of the experience of intrusive thoughts—the thoughts just don't seem as "loud"

- Increasing the threshold at which a person goes from being anxious to being panicked

- Decreasing the likelihood of slipping from disappointment to depression

- Increasing the ability to tolerate exposure, thus improving the effectiveness of ERP

This last point is significant. Many people with OCD who are considering medication worry that meds will make their exposure therapy ineffective, by making them unafraid. What really happens is that an increase in fear tolerance aided by meds makes a person more capable of engaging in meaningful exposures without panicking. In my clinical experience, this is ultimately what makes the difference. With or without medication, it's ERP over time that spells mastery over OCD.

Current psychiatric approaches to OCD include a variety of medications that affect neurotransmitters other than serotonin. Despite the overall efficacy of SSRIs, 40 to 60 percent of OCD sufferers do not benefit much or at all from an SSRI alone (McDougle et al. 1993). It may be helpful to combine small doses of *atypical antipsychotics* (such as Seroquel and Risperdal, which act on the neurotransmitter dopamine) with an SSRI (Skapinakis, Papatheodorou, and Maureas 2007). Medications like memantine (Namenda), which affect the neurotransmitter glutamate, also may have a therapeutic effect (Haghighi et al. 2013).

Treating the Unwanted Intrusion in Your Family

Just as your family member is struggling with unwanted mental intrusions, you and your whole family are struggling with the unwanted intrusion of the OCD itself. Your family member's OCD shows up at the least convenient times, interfering in your ability to focus on the present moment and enjoy life. Maybe your family member's OCD got in the way of a special event, such as a wedding or a birthday party. Maybe it gets in the way of otherwise quiet family moments, like dinnertime or watching TV.

When something triggers your family member's OCD, do you turn away from her coldly when you see her squirm? Sometimes you have to. Or do you help her out of her predicament by accommodating some ritual? Sometimes you have to. Will you wash or avoid with her just to keep the peace? And what about the sacrifices you make to keep the peace for the rest of your family? You're in an unenviable position. Let's say your son has Contamination OCD, and he sees you accidentally touch the tines of his fork while setting the table. You know that just getting him another fork will ensure a peaceful meal. But while you're doing that, the rest of your family will be waiting to eat, growing increasingly frustrated. Plus, then he'll need a new fork every time his OCD demands it. Do you tell him to just get over it, then? How will that work out? You just can't win. So although your family member needs to take responsibility for fighting his OCD, you have a fight against OCD too.

In part 2 of this book, you'll learn some ways to navigate the OCD maze with your family member. As you do, I encourage you to reflect on the basic tenets of cognitive behavioral treatment for OCD—how they apply to your loved one, but also how they apply to *your* battle with your family member's disorder. On the cognitive front, how are your distorted thoughts about the situation pushing you to accommodate your family member's compulsions? How might your distorted thinking be increasing your own discomfort, your resentment of having to deal with your family member's OCD?

When you stop offering reassurance and participating in other rituals, your family member with OCD will be in pain, and he'll let you know it. He may even blame you for it. "All you have to do is answer this one question and I'll leave you alone!" he may say. He may even believe it. Watching your family member suffer is just as painful for you as anything your family member is going through, but you need to keep things in perspective. Whenever my young daughter accidentally collides with a toilet paper holder (because they tend to be right at a four-year-old's eye level), she cries as if it's the end of the world. I hate it, but I know when her pain subsides—and it will—mine will too. Your family member with OCD is grappling with a thought or a feeling or a sensation that cuts to the core of his being, and he may not believe it'll ever stop. The OCD clouds his ability to see the impermanence of pain. That means he considers suffering indefinitely and is trying to cope both with what he fears and with the idea that he may fear it forever. So to ride out discomfort with him, knowing that all you have to do is participate in a compulsion to give him some relief, will take great strength.

Just as your family member needs to learn how to accept uncertainty and the presence of unwanted thoughts, you have to learn to cope with her OCD nonjudgmentally. Throughout the second part of this book, consider how mindfulness can help you cope with the challenges of addressing your family member's OCD. But also think about how you can apply mindfulness when faced with other stressors—for example, when you're stuck in traffic or when you get that call from school that your son has been in the bathroom for the last hour and won't come out.

The Myth That It's All About You

It's reasonable to acknowledge the drama in your own life that your loved one's OCD is causing. It's impossible to overlook all the times you couldn't leave the house on time because he insisted that you wait for him to finish rituals, couldn't enjoy watching TV because he kept asking questions or demanding control of the remote, or couldn't enjoy a nice home-cooked meal because something you prepared triggered his OCD. He's self-absorbed—literally. He's absorbed in himself, in his obsessions and compulsions. Quite frankly, *his* problem is in *your* way, and you probably imagine that when he changes for the better, you'll change for the better.

That's partially true. Whether you're the parent, the spouse, the sibling, or the child of someone with OCD, someone else's mental health issue is affecting your life. All that person needs to do is recognize this, and she'll stop being that way, right? Unfortunately, no. The most common thing I hear from OCD sufferers when discussing how their OCD affects their family is that the guilt is so painful they can't handle bringing it into focus. Thoughts of how their "failure" to resist compulsions is actually causing other people pain become another unwanted intrusion.

Acknowledging the pain your family member with OCD is in doesn't mean dismissing your own pain. What it means is that you and your loved one with OCD both feel a pain, and both have the opportunity to overcome or master the source of that pain together. It's not all about you and how *her* OCD interfered in *your* life. It's about you and your family and how OCD has become a part of it.

The Myth That It Doesn't Affect You

The relentless turmoil inside OCD sufferers' heads can often create somewhat of a paradox. On one hand, they're overwhelmed by a seemingly endless empathy, constantly thinking about other people's feelings and what those feelings may lead to. Someone with Contamination OCD may think: *If I don't wash my hands, I might spread germs, which might get someone sick, and they may feel pain. Then I'll feel pain knowing I caused it. I'll feel their pain and my pain. Better to wash.* Or someone with Harm OCD may have a thought of hurting a loved one, accompanied by a very clear image of the loved one in pain and a very clear sense of the severity of her pain, to the extent that the urge to avoid relating to that pain pushes him to ritualize. And yet, being so caught up in it all makes him completely unaware of the pain his OCD itself is causing his family members.

"Why do you care so much if I get therapy? It's not as if it affects you," your family member with OCD may say. But of course it does affect you. It affects you in many ways. There are the obvious accommodations you feel you must make in consideration of your loved one's OCD. You try not to upset her, try not to talk about the wrong things, try not to interfere in her rituals, et cetera, et cetera. But there's also the toll it takes on you. Your family member might believe that you can't tell when she's "in her head," but you *can*. You know her all too well. You know *that* look. And how does that look affect you? Are any of the following thoughts familiar to you?

- *He doesn't respect me enough to share what he's thinking and feeling. He doesn't think I can handle it.*

- *She doesn't value my time* (while you're waiting for her to finish ritualizing).

- *He doesn't turn to me in need. I'm not good enough.*

- *I'm a poor excuse for a family member. She's suffering, and I'm just watching, helpless.*

- *He doesn't care that I feel abandoned, left out of the secret party in his head.*

- *I did something wrong. I don't know what, but something I said or did set her off, and now it's going to be a terrible day.*

- *Home isn't safe. He might start obsessing over something.*

These internalized messages affect you and, just like obsessive thoughts, can eat away at your self-esteem, your motivation, and your confidence. They can cause anxiety, fatigue, and depression. These effects will worsen unless you address them, and often they require approaches similar to treatment for OCD.

Consider This

So now you know how OCD is treated: with CBT, ERP, mindfulness, and medication. You've just read about a number of things your family member can do to overcome his OCD. But he's still the one who has to do them. And they all may be terrifying. Exposure to fears? Resisting compulsions? Accepting thoughts without judgment? Medication? Sure, they work, but they require commitment to a protracted uphill battle. Take a moment to picture your family member standing at the foot of a mountain, looking up toward a peak he can't even see through the clouds.

Your Struggle

In the next part of this book, you'll learn how to recognize, cope with, and help fight specific compulsions your family member may be struggling with. I just dumped a ton of information on you, so take a break before you head into part 2. Supporting a family member with OCD requires that you pace yourself. You can't fix the problem immediately; you have to give it consistent effort over time. This often requires getting used to doing less, not more.

Part 2

Supporting Your Family Member with OCD

In chapters 4 through 9, I discuss a few common compulsions and how you can better understand and help your loved one address them. The strategies in these chapters are meant to apply in any type of family relationship—parent-child, spousal, sibling, and so on. Although in chapters 10 and 11, I discuss strategies that are specific to certain kinds of family members (children, partners, parents, and siblings), I recommend you read each of the following chapters first. Even if your family member doesn't seem to engage in the particular compulsion that the chapter focuses on, the strategies discussed for helping and coping with it may prove useful with other compulsions, especially any not covered in this book. In each chapter, you'll find a list of the ways each compulsion may show up for different obsessions. Know that this is by no means an exhaustive list, and not every compulsion can be represented here for each obsession.

Chapter 4

Accommodation and the Four I's Approach

Accommodation is the very foundation of family. The word "accommodation" means "settlement," "arrangement," or "compromise." When my wife and I moved in together, we had to make arrangements for fitting two people's possessions into one space, by discarding certain possessions and moving others around until everything fit. When we had our first child, we had to settle on turning what would have been a guest room or an office into a child's bedroom. When we had our second child, we had to modify our first child's bedroom to accommodate her little sister. And those are just examples of accommodations for space. All the other settlements and arrangements that keep my family whole require that each of us does or doesn't do different things on a regular basis so that everyone's needs are met. Some accommodations are easy, and some are quite taxing. I recently started accommodating my older daughter's need to get to school by sacrificing about another 20 minutes of precious sleep each morning. But most accommodations are actually quite enjoyable, such as making space on the couch for all of us on movie night.

So what do people do when a family member expresses a new need? Naturally, we accommodate it, often before we even consider whether this "need" is real or imaginary. People are conditioned to associate accommodation of the needs of a loved one with the reward of peaceful cohabitation. But few anticipate that a family member's needs will *grow* with accommodation, and as those needs grow, he'll demand more accommodation and the family system will begin to implode. This is the pain of the OCD family. There's a hole in the system and a nearly unlimited supply of accommodation to fill that hole, but suddenly the rules have changed. Now that OCD has joined the family, accommodation becomes the problem.

Accommodation of OCD symptoms is very common among family members, and catching and addressing accommodation early may increase the odds of treatment success (Gomes et al. 2014). Furthermore, the greater the family's accommodation of OCD symptoms, the greater the family's stress and dysfunction overall, including resentment and rejection of the OCD sufferer (Steketee and Van Noppen 2003).

Family accommodation comes in many forms, including changing the family routine and becoming directly involved in compulsions (Torres et al. 2012). You may be accommodating by waiting for rituals to be completed, avoiding doing things that might trigger your family member's OCD, or even washing, checking, or doing other rituals yourself at your family member's request. A recent meta-analysis of family involvement in OCD treatment found that treatments specifically meant to reduce family accommodation correlated with greater patient improvement (Thompson-Hollands et al. 2014).

Think of accommodation as making arrangements for the OCD to stay in the family. By reducing accommodation safely and with consideration of your family member's pain, you can make it clear that OCD is not a welcome guest in your loved one's mind or in your home.

The Four I's of Helping a Family Member with OCD

As self-help authors tend to do, I've thought of an easy way to help you remember some important steps. I call it "the four I's" (no offense to anyone who wears glasses!):

1. **Identify** the compulsion, not the person, as the problem.

2. **Invite** collaboration.

3. **Interrupt** the obsessive-compulsive cycle (with permission).

4. **Integrate** and model healthy behavior.

No single strategy is a guarantee that you'll be able to help your family member with OCD. But these four steps can point you in the right direction, so that you at least do no harm.

Identify the Compulsion, Not the Person, as the Problem

One thing is abundantly clear when it comes to OCD—hostile criticism doesn't work. In fact, some kinds of criticism may have a negative effect (Renshaw, Steketee, and Chambless 2005). You might feel frustrated with your family member when you see him engage in the same nonsensical compulsions over and over again. You might think, *What's wrong with him?* But so long as you're pressuring him to change who he is, you're not helping him overcome the OCD. It's not about who he is. It's about what he feels compelled to do and how he responds to those urges. If your family member is engaging in compulsions, chances are he truly feels it's important to do so (even if intellectually it defies logic).

His pain is real. It doesn't matter that the pain is triggered by a false alarm in his brain. It's still an alarm to him.

So the first thing you can do to help a loved one with OCD is identify the *behavior* as problematic, not the person. For example, if your wife is compulsively checking that the curling iron is off, and this interferes with your ability to get out the door on time, it's the checking that's the problem, not your wife. Point out how the behavior is interfering in the things your wife cares about or how it's causing her to miss out on opportunities. Given that waiting for her and being late is a problem for you, how is it also a problem for *her*? Maybe she doesn't like being late either. Try to help her identify what she's missing out on because of this behavior, so that the two of you are on the same team, fighting against the OCD instead of fighting with each other.

Invite Collaboration

For the most part, this book presumes that your family member either is already in treatment or is interested in self-treatment. The tools I discuss are unlikely to work for someone who hasn't acknowledged that he has OCD or that it's treatable. In most cases of OCD, improvement won't occur until the OCD sufferer is interested in getting better and is willing to do the work; forcing treatment upon him is likely to result only in conflict. If your family member doesn't yet seem open to the idea that change is possible, you may have to wait and focus on your own coping skills and stress management for now. For example, if you have a child who's especially resistant to acknowledging her OCD, it's important that you focus on yourself, either through personal psychotherapy or through some other means of support.

If your family member has recognized his compulsive behavior as problematic, however, the logical next step is inviting him to work on it. It must be an invitation, not an order. Ordering him to "stop it" is a form of character indictment that will result in more anxiety and often defiant protection of the rituals (the opposite of what you want). However, inviting him to work on something together, for everyone's benefit, can come without personal judgment and shame. You've identified that the compulsion is problematic. Now you can ask: "Would you like to try to change it? Can I help? Can we do this together?" This step is essential, because so many compulsive behaviors in a family context *rely* on other members of the family system to keep the symptoms going. If your family member compulsively seeks reassurance, she has to make an effort to stop seeking it; but also you have to make an effort to stop giving it, otherwise the cycle will continue. In order for a family member to help a loved one with OCD, there needs to be a self-propelled effort on the part of the person with OCD, bolstered by a team effort.

Interrupt the Obsessive-Compulsive Cycle (with Permission)

Once the problem has been identified and defined, and your family member has accepted your invitation to work on it, the next step is to actually get in the way of your family member's OCD. By that, I mean reducing accommodation and interfering in her ability to perform compulsions.

To do this without permission is likely to be seen as a punishment, which will only drive sneakier, more manipulative compulsions. For example, if your wife who's a compulsive hand-washer has not agreed to let you take all the soap away, she'll simply buy more soap if you do (or switch to hand sanitizer). But if the two of you agree that removing the soap from the bathroom will help reduce her hand-washing, then there's a context for the pain it will cause.

This step is where you'll be the most involved in using cognitive behavioral tools to help your family member. You'll identify a goal and create a hierarchy of exposures and other behavioral changes that lead to that goal. You'll reinforce mindfulness concepts and at times challenge your family member's distorted thinking. If your family member is in treatment, let it be known that you're interested in sitting in on a session and getting educated on how to help your loved one. Though you can't force your way into the therapy, you can be vocal about your support, and most therapists will welcome the opportunity to teach you how to reinforce healthy behaviors at home. If therapy isn't in the picture, you may be able to use a workbook (see the resources) to the same end. Just be careful not to slip into the role of therapist. You are what you are. If you're a dad whose son has OCD, be a dad who helps his son fight OCD—don't be his therapist.

Resist the urge to experiment on your family member or show her how "easy" it is to not do compulsions. Instead, start by asking your family member what you can do to help and how you can intervene. It's also in this step, the "interrupt" step, that you should look at ways in which you're accommodating your family member's rituals and start phasing them out. Think back to the "invite" step, and see whether you and your family member can construct a hierarchy or timeline for this process together. You may be surprised how much your family member actually *wants* you to stop accommodating or wants you to get in the way of her OCD but is afraid to volunteer. It takes a kind of "selling out" of the OCD's secrets for her to ask you to snap her out of it if you see her doing a ritual. If she lets you know how to help, she's already resisting the OCD, and that means the OCD may take "revenge" in the form of some *other* unwanted thought. So try to remember that she's much like a political dissident seeking asylum from an oppressive dictatorship (her OCD) and you're an ambassador from the free world. Letting you know how to sneak her out of OCD country takes tremendous bravery.

Integrate and Model Healthy Behaviors

You've identified the problem, contracted to work together on solving it, and started reducing accommodation and helping your family member block himself from compulsive behaviors that are fueling his obsessions. But the mere absence of compulsions won't result in mastery over OCD, because it leaves a vacuum that will just be filled with other dysfunctional behaviors. A family member who typically spends three hours in the shower (some people with OCD spend even longer) may let you shut the water off after an agreed-upon time limit. That will help. But what will she do with the rest of that time? Left to her own devices, she'll find other ways of getting that clean feeling. To get better, she'll have to learn to tolerate feeling unclean while engaging in more meaningful (non-compulsive) behavior. As a supportive family member, you can take a leadership role in giving her something to do, something to attend to, something that accounts for her time away from compulsions. Ask the average OCD sufferer what he has lost to OCD, and the first thing he'll tell you is "time."

You can further promote healthy behaviors by modeling them yourself. This can be as simple as starting an exercise routine or a new hobby and inviting your family member to join you. Modeling healthy exposure can be useful too. If your family member is having a hard time with exposure to a certain TV show, start watching a TV show that makes *you* feel uncomfortable. If your family member is compulsively washing between activities, cut down your own washing. Just remember to do this not as a taunt, but as a show of alliance against the OCD. As a therapist, I always ensure that I'm asking a client to do only what I myself would be willing to do. Much to the dismay of my clients (until they get better, that is), I'm willing to do a lot of peculiar things. By demonstrating your own willingness to be uncomfortable, you'll help your family member realize he can confront his discomfort and sit with it instead of going back to doing compulsions.

Consider This

If your family member has acknowledged that OCD is a problem in his life, then he wants you to understand it. He wants you to see that he's more than his OCD. But being told something is wrong with your brain takes more than a little getting used to. To your family member, your offer of help might feel as though a doctor is showing him an image of his disordered brain and saying, "We're just gonna do a tiny bit of SURGERY right here in this problem area." It might seem scary. Nobody wants to be a family member's guinea pig, so be gentle, be patient, and be kind.

Your Struggle

Tempting as it would've been to title this book How to Stop Your Family Member from Having OCD, *stopping your family member from having OCD is simply not feasible. The suggestions and strategies above represent ways to engage your family member with OCD and try to lovingly nudge him in the direction of better mental health. As the saying goes, "You can lead a horse to water, but you can't make him drink." You can lead your loved one away from rituals, but he has to do the work of exposing himself to his triggers. By using the four I's (identify, invite, interrupt, integrate), you can position yourself as an essential reinforcement of healthy behavior. But nothing is a cure-all, so be patient, be gentle, and be kind to yourself.*

Chapter 5

When Your Family Member Is Avoiding

The fundamental problem with avoidance of the things that make us uncomfortable is that it causes our brains to learn the wrong message. When we avoid something, we believe we're telling ourselves that we're safe. But the brain uses a kind of opposite language. It calculates meaning based on *explanations* of behavior. When we avoid something, the only reasonable explanation is that whatever it is we're avoiding must be dangerous. So, for example, when your family member with OCD begins to avoid shaking hands with people for fear of germs, she's sending a powerful message to her brain that shaking hands with people is indeed inherently dangerous and the threat she perceives is real. The truth, however, is that her obsessions are just meaningless glitches.

One of my favorite quotes from Pema Chödrön's eye-opening book *The Wisdom of No Escape* is "There's a common misunderstanding among all the human beings who have ever been born on the earth that the best way to live life is to try to avoid pain and just try to get comfortable" (1991, 1). Avoidance of pain comes naturally to us. It's in our DNA, programming us to associate pain with danger, danger with death, and death with something to be avoided at all costs.

Avoidance of things that are upsetting to you is essentially rational, except when the upset is caused by a false alarm, as in OCD. For example, it makes sense to avoid touching something that you believe might give you a disease, if there's concrete evidence that it might give you a disease. But what if you believed that touching it might give you a disease even though there's no concrete evidence? In the OCD mind, the thoughts about risk are loud and distorted. The question stops being one of "How much do I believe?" and becomes one of "How far do I need to go to protect myself and my loved ones from danger?"

The other issue with avoidance has to do with degrees of avoidance. To illustrate degrees of avoidance: I'm not a huge fan of snakes. If I see a snake, I'll back away, giving it as much space as it may need to move erratically and suddenly at someone else, thank you very much! This is avoidance in the first degree: avoidance of direct contact. If, due to my fear of snakes, I were to also avoid lakes or grassy areas where snakes might be present, that's an additional degree of avoidance. And if I had an obsessive fear of snakes, something several degrees removed from an actual snake (such as a picture of a snake, or the letter *s*) might bring my fear to mind, and the presence of this fear would trigger an urge to avoid. If I responded to that urge, I'd feel safer (even though there's no danger of my being bitten by the letter *s*). Once I felt relief—*click*, my brain would get the negative reinforcement cue and record that avoidance of the letter *s* is a good thing. I'd begin to see the letter as being much closer to an actual snake than I intellectually know it is.

Some avoidance requires no accommodation from loved ones. Let's say your family member with OCD doesn't watch certain kinds of movies anymore or doesn't wear the color green. Who cares, right? But since every family is a system, made up of moving parts that take energy from each other and give energy back, even small avoidant behaviors can eventually cause a rift in the system. If Dad stops taking out the trash because of his contamination fears, Mom may simply take over that chore. But if Mom is now taking five minutes to take out the trash, she may not feel like spending an extra five minutes helping Junior with his homework. Junior then feels unsupported and starts acting out by picking a fight with his sister. Suddenly everyone is at each other's throats and nobody really knows why.

It gets even more complicated. Mom knows that Dad obsesses for hours every time he takes out the trash because he can't seem to convince himself that he's clean enough to handle the baby afterward. If she insists he continue doing this seemingly simple five-minute chore (taking out the trash), she has to deal with his sour mood and general avoidance for hours afterward, during which time *she* has to give the baby a bath, help Junior with his homework, and so on. Suddenly, again, everyone is fighting and nobody knows why. So Mom tries to avoid conflict by just taking out the trash herself, but she doesn't realize that it leads to conflict anyway. More importantly, she may not see how it validates in Dad's mind that the trash is dangerous and should be avoided, ultimately resulting in a worsening of his OCD and more conflict.

Why Your Family Member May Be Avoiding

All obsessions typically involve attempts to avoid triggering situations, even if only attempts to avoid thinking unwanted thoughts. For frame of reference, Starcevic et al. (2011) found that 80 percent of people with Contamination OCD and 50 percent of people with aggressive obsessions (Harm OCD) engaged in compulsive avoidance.

Things People with OCD Commonly Avoid

(Listed by type of obsessions)

Contamination obsessions

- Items used by the general public, such as doorknobs, remotes, handrails, and public restrooms

- Items associated with poison, chemicals, or pesticide (such as household cleaners)

- Sticky substances—anything that might cause contaminants to stick to the skin

- Household chores that involve contact with "contaminated" things

- Tasks that involve being responsible for cleaning things

- Cross-contamination (for example, avoiding touching "clean" bedsheets after having touched "dirty" laundry)

Hyper-responsibility (checking) obsessions

- Responsibility for turning appliances off or locking doors

- Potentially (or seemingly) dangerous tasks, such as driving and cooking

Just Right obsessions

- Schoolwork, business tasks, or anything that may encourage attempts at perfection

- Household chores that may be difficult to do perfectly (such as washing dishes)

Violent obsessions

- Items that could be used as weapons (such as knives, pencils, or anything sharp)

- Violence in the media (such as news articles and violent films)

- Anyone perceived as vulnerable, such as children or the elderly—even a spouse or sibling if associated with violent thoughts

- Public places or anywhere that may trigger thoughts of "snapping" and harming strangers

Sexual obsessions

- Children (in the case of pedophilia obsessions)

- "Attractive" people of a certain sex (in the case of sexual orientation obsessions)

- Any form of intimacy or closeness (such as sitting next to the person who's the focus of the obsessions)

- Music, media, or fashion associated with a feared sexual identity

Relationship obsessions

- Making plans for the future (as small as a date or as big as a vacation)

- Intimacy

- Indicators of commitment to the relationship (such as spending time with each other's families)

- Social activities that could trigger thoughts about being single

Religious obsessions

- Places of worship

- Religious texts

- Blogs, books, shows, or movies with religious themes

Moral obsessions

- News stories about "immoral" acts

- Blogs, books, shows, or movies with morality as a theme

- Tasks that call into question one's intentions (for example, holding a baby may bring up the question of why the baby was held a particular way and whether the placement of the hands on the baby was appropriate)

If it seems odd to you that such seemingly innocuous things would warrant the effort it takes to avoid them, it means that your family member with OCD is having an experience with these things that's different from what you experience. You see a bread knife, but she sees a reminder that she may be a serial killer. You see a scuff mark on the wall, but she sees a potentially disease-spreading contaminant. In other words, you see what things *are*, but your family member with OCD sees what things *could* be. If she was thinking *mindfully*, she'd be able to observe that she was simply having thoughts about what things could be. But, mired in anxiety and fear, she sees only danger. The more she avoids the danger, the more dangerous it seems.

Empathy for your family member with OCD can, ironically, keep you from doing what's most helpful to her. If you perceived that your loved one felt as if she was in danger, then your instinct would typically be to accommodate avoidance, to "help" your family member escape dealing with something. After all, why let someone you love suffer, even if the danger isn't real? But besides the ripple effect this has on the rest of your family, it doesn't do your family member with OCD the favor you'd hope for. When you accommodate avoidance, you're teaming up with the OCD to tell your family member that the feared thing really *is* dangerous *and* he's not capable of confronting it. He then comes to rely upon the accommodation, and your relationship to him changes: you become a tool of his OCD, facilitating his compulsions and perpetuating his distorted thinking.

Identify the Compulsion, Not the Person, as the Problem

Tempting though it may be, in most cases it won't work to simply force your family member to stop avoiding things, certainly not all at once. Throwing someone in the deep end not only fails to teach good swimming technique, it sends the message that you don't care whether she drowns. So what can you do?

First, you and your family member need to agree that there's a problem to solve. Both of you have to be willing to identify the OCD as the culprit. If your message is "You can't keep avoiding this thing" or "I'm sick of doing this for you," then it misses the point. Your family member doesn't relish in avoidance because it's convenient for him. He *relies* on avoidance because of a belief that interaction with his triggers will annihilate him. But this belief is caused by the disorder, so if the two of you can agree that the disorder is the problem, then you can address the problem with less conflict.

Your annoyance at your family member's avoidance of triggers won't be enough to motivate him to face his fears. So there needs to be a meaningful personal goal. If the two of you put your heads together, I'm sure you'll find your family member's avoidance of triggers is somehow keeping him from doing what's important to him. Let's say your daughter is avoiding swimming with her little sister in the backyard pool because of a fear that chemicals in the water will give her cancer. Is she really missing out on only a dip in the pool—a little pointless recreation? What about the interaction with her sister? If she joined her sister in the pool, maybe they'd throw a ball around, race laps, and play Marco Polo. Maybe her sister would learn about fair play. Maybe she'd learn how to do a cannonball and get the biggest splash. Whatever her sister learned would be a result of that interaction with *her*. With that perspective, the issue is no longer about the pool and avoiding fears associated with the pool. It's about being somebody's big sister. Values, such as being the best big sister possible, are the key to meaningful goals. If it matters to your daughter (in this example) to be a good big sister, then there's a reason for her to fight compulsions that affect her interactions with her little sister.

Invite Collaboration

If your family member accepts that her avoidance is coming from the OCD, and she agrees that this avoidance is interfering with living her life according to her values, then she'll be motivated to stop avoiding. But if she's accustomed to letting the OCD have its way, and you're accustomed to accommodating, it won't be easy for either of you to suddenly shift to nonavoidance. Your family member will have to overcome avoidance by degrees. In the example above, perhaps your daughter will find it too overwhelming to immerse herself in the pool. Can she sit next to the pool long enough to throw a ball back and forth? Work with your family member to come up with a plan that chips away at the avoidance.

The same rules apply for accommodation. If you're assuming full responsibility for changing diapers because your husband with violent or sexual obsessions can't bear to be around a naked baby, you'll have to come up with a plan that reduces how much responsibility you assume for changing diapers while increasing how much he steps in to do at whatever level of discomfort he's willing to tolerate to reclaim the value of being an involved father.

When a Family Member Has OCD

Sometimes OCD sufferers' avoidance has become so ingrained that they don't even know what they're avoiding anymore. They've been treading a cautious, winding path around their triggers for so long, it feels like the normal one. To bring the avoidance back into your family member's awareness, you may have to point it out. This will be tricky, because every time you point out an avoidance (or any compulsion), you're essentially saying, "I know more about what's going on than you do." So that this unfortunate dynamic doesn't always lead to conflict, try to find a tone that doesn't sound too condescending and a way of phrasing what you want to say gently so that it doesn't sound like "Gotcha!" Remember, you're the expert on your family member, but your family member is the expert on her subjective emotional experience. So ask her in advance: "Do you want me to point out when you're avoiding? When are good times to point out that you're avoiding? How do you want me to point out that you're avoiding?" Maybe your family member would prefer you to be passive and concrete: "Hey, I noticed you seem to be trying not to touch that." Maybe she'd prefer you to be more direct: "Hey, that's your OCD. Can you try something different?" If simply hearing "OCD" or being told that she's symptomatic is too shameful, it may be best to agree on a code word, like "platypus." This is where knowing your family member (the person, not the disorder) will make a meaningful difference.

Interrupt the Obsessive-Compulsive Cycle (with Permission)

Getting a grip on the OCD may be reward enough, but maybe not. If your family member has agreed that the problem is OCD, has acknowledged that his avoidance is interfering in the pursuit of a meaningful value, and has worked with you to plan a gradual stop to avoidance and accommodation, he stands a chance at improving. But it's hard work and can feel demoralizing. It's an uphill battle, against the wind, in the rain.

Highlighting the positive and recognizing nonavoidance goes a long way. For adults, a reward can be as simple as a "thank you" or any open acknowledgement of effort. For children, a sticker chart or point system may be more meaningful, with every step toward their goal bringing them that much closer to a new toy or a trip to Disneyland.

Once you've identified and agreed to target the avoidance, you can start getting in the way. In most cases this means doing less. If your family member wants to avoid touching the door and waits for you to open it for him, then (with his permission), you can wait behind him and act as if you assume he'll open the door for you. Start watching what *you* want to watch on TV, whether he's there or not. Instead of changing the channel in order to keep him in the room, let him make the decision to stay and sit with the discomfort. Stop avoiding the use of trigger words (or numbers or colors). This doesn't mean you should go out of your way to trigger his OCD (though you can if you're invited to), but, basically, stop walking on eggshells.

Your family member may verbalize his resistance to ending avoidance, telling you things like "I can't be around that! I'll lose it!" This is a distorted belief and represents catastrophic thinking. You can encourage healthy restructuring without reassurance by responding: "It's really hard for you to be around that. I don't know how you'll handle it, but I'm here for you when you're ready to try."

Integrate and Model Healthy Behaviors

By demonstrating your own nonavoidance (including nonavoidance of your family member's distress), you'll set the stage for

Mindfulness Tip

Avoidance is an urge. An urge is an internal experience, like a thought or a feeling. Rather than encouraging your family member to ignore it or pretend it doesn't exist, support the idea that she can acknowledge that the urge is present in her mind and body without letting it control her. The same goes for you. Notice your own urges to "fix" your family member and "get her better." Though your heart is in the right place, being driven by these urges won't likely bring about the results you're looking for.

change. If your family member had been avoiding doing the dishes and you no longer have to assume that responsibility for her, don't just sit and watch her do the dishes. Do something with your new-found time as well. Seeing the family functioning better as a whole can be a great motivator for her.

Especially with avoidance, it may not be so easy to tell how hard your family member with OCD is working to overcome the disorder. If he has Just Right OCD and starts sitting at the kitchen table without shifting his chair a certain number of times, it may just look, well, normal. In other words, you won't always feel a strong urge to comment positively when your family member abstains from rituals. However, you may feel a strong urge to criticize when he engages in rituals. So if your family member is working on reducing avoidance—whether with your participation, under the guidance of a therapist, or on his own—talk to him about what level of feedback he'd appreciate. He may want recognition for his hard work resisting compulsions. Or he may find recognition to be condescending or triggering, no matter how nicely you put it. Work with him on incentives, whether praise or material rewards, for resisting compulsions. If, through treatment, he's able to see that avoidance and accommodation don't help, he'll be the only one who can tell you what really does help.

If your family member is doing ERP, whether with an OCD specialist or on her own, she very likely will have to confront some disturbing things on a regular basis. Some of these things (touching publicly used items without washing, viewing violent movies, and leaving clothes imperfectly folded, to name a few) may seem like good things for anyone to avoid. The best thing you can do to help your family member with OCD is empathize with her pain and, in some cases, participate in behaviors you too would typically avoid. If it bothers you to walk around with "germy" hands, imagine what your family member is attempting to tolerate. Then consider what it might mean to your family member if you helped her set the dinner table with unclean hands. Go ahead and watch that horror movie (it's okay to cover your eyes, but try not to!) and let your family member see you out of your comfort zone. Reassurance doesn't work, it's true. But making tolerance of discomfort look achievable is comforting, and that's perfectly acceptable!

When to Accommodate Avoidance

Should you ever accommodate avoidance of things that trigger your family member's OCD? It depends on how entrenched your family member has become in avoiding those things. If avoidance is caught early, then the answer is to never accommodate. This doesn't mean you should ever force your family member to face her triggers (such as forcing a child to go on an amusement park ride she is afraid will break); rather, it means making a concrete choice about how to respond to a compulsive demand. Let's say you're watching TV together and a commercial comes on about a sale on children's clothing. Your family member with intrusive thoughts about being a danger to children requests that you change the channel immediately, and you know his history of struggling with this obsession. If he hasn't roped you into accommodating his compulsive avoidance already, don't let him start.

You can use any number of tactics to resist accommodating avoidance. Mostly it's an issue of timing: he wants you to act urgently because the experience he's having is urgent. You can reject the urgency by moving slowly—for example, waiting to reply to his request to change the channel long enough that by the time you reach for the remote, the commercial is over.

It may be obvious to you that OCD is driving the avoidance, but calling it out—"That's your OCD!"—might trigger more anxiety, and you might end up with an angry family member leaving the room to do compulsions on her own. Something more supportive, like "It'll be over soon" or "I know that's hard to watch right now," might be more effective and still delay the accommodation long enough that it becomes less urgent.

If your family member is asking you to accommodate her avoidance of a complex task (such as a household chore), nip it in the bud. Literally refuse to do it the first time she asks, and literally give up whatever it is you need to give up while waiting for her to accept that she'll have to do something that bothers her.

All this being said, once the cycle (intrusive thought, compulsive avoidance, then demanding accommodation to continue avoidance) has started, you have to extract yourself gradually. If you try to stop the cycle all at once, your family member's avoidance ritual will simply be replaced with more rituals and more conflict. So sometimes you'll have to figure out how to be less of an accomplice to your family member's avoidance while still accommodating it to some extent. You'll have to extract yourself as he works on extracting himself. This will take time and require a plan. Map it out. Determine what you'll continue to help him avoid and for how long, with a partnership agreement to eliminate avoidance and accommodation related to the obsession.

Let's say your family member has long avoided opening doors, for fear of being contaminated by other people's germs. This has left you with the responsibility of opening all doors for him, which may prove inconvenient for a number of reasons. A sudden refusal to open doors for him may result in a standoff, which you'll lose because in such moments your family member is simply willing to sacrifice more for the OCD than for your convenience. If on the other hand the two of you agree to work on this problem, you can make a plan in which you move from step to step as distress becomes more manageable and accommodation has ceased. For example:

1. You open all doors that require the touch of a hand, but he opens all doors that don't (for example, using his back or side to push the door open).

2. He places his hand on top of yours when you open doors.

3. He opens doors using his sleeve or a napkin.

4. You give him a set amount of time to consider opening the door with his hands while you wait, after which, if he feels unable, you'll accommodate.

5. You open only every fifth door.

6. You have him open all doors for you.

The length of a plan like this is flexible, with you and your family member collaborating on when to move on to the next step. Generally, you should practice each step until your family member's discomfort level starts to go down, but it's not necessary to wait for total comfort before moving on to the next challenge.

Consider This

Throughout this entire process, remember that the thing your family member with OCD is avoiding feels threatening to her. It's not laziness that drives her avoidance; it's fear. It doesn't matter to her brain that the fear is based on distorted beliefs—fear is pain, and human instinct is to avoid pain. Remember, too, that your family member probably feels a lot of shame about asking you to pick up the slack in areas she's avoiding because of her OCD. Consider what it must feel like to need someone to do things for you because you're too afraid.

Your Struggle

The reality is that you can't fix your family member's problem. Your role is to support your family member in fixing it himself. He may not be ready or may not believe it's fixable. You're stuck between (a) inviting or allowing pain for your loved one by refusing to accommodate avoidance and (b) allowing avoidance to continue spiraling out of control until your loved one is incapable of functioning. How can you choose between these two seemingly unacceptable states? In the end, it comes down to accepting what you can and can't control as much as what you can and can't tolerate. Rather than judge yourself on how successful you've been at helping your family member not avoid his triggers, and rather than being critical of the successes yet to come, try to focus on how much emphasis you've put on being supportive of his mental health efforts.

Chapter 6

When a Family Member Is Seeking Reassurance and Confessing

We give them different names, but compulsions really are just variations on the same insatiable quest for certainty that something bad won't happen and that the pain of anxiety will go away. In some ways, an OCD sufferer who's asking for reassurance that his fears aren't true is trying to purge his mind of an unwanted thought. An OCD sufferer's compulsive hand-washing is an attempt to get reassurance that his hands aren't in a dangerous state of uncleanliness. An OCD sufferer who checks to make sure the stove is off is really just obtaining visual reassurance that the stove knob is in the off position.

Reassurance

Reassurance-seeking is a common compulsive behavior that can be a serious burden on the family (Williams et al. 2011). It's best understood by breaking down the word itself. An *assurance* is a promise that instills confidence. Let's say you're trying to get someone to loan you money. You promise, "I assure you I'll pay you back as soon as I get my paycheck." *Should I lend him money?* the other person thinks. *How do I know he'll pay me back? Well, he assured me he will.* By adding "re-" to the word, we're essentially saying "promise again," with the intent of instilling more confidence and, ultimately, the illusion of certainty.

The OCD sufferer is involved in a negotiation whenever an obsession is present. Typically speaking, she doesn't *want* to do exhausting, pointless, self-perpetuating rituals. She's seeking a way around that, but there's pain involved and she wants to get away from that pain. Reassurance is a way of negotiating away from the burden of accepting uncertainty, by getting someone else to vouch for her safety. To use the example above, it's like getting someone to cover your debt in case your paycheck doesn't come through. In OCD terms, it means getting the outside world to guarantee that an obsession won't come true.

Most reassurance-seeking takes the form of questions. "Is that dirty?" "Can this make me sick?" "Does this mean I'm gay?" "Would you love me if I went insane?" "Are you sure the stove is turned off?" "Would you think I was 'bad' if I _____?" Reassurance-seeking may also take the form of research, especially on the Internet—asking the opinions of strangers on online forums, scouring medical websites for symptoms, and so on. People who are seeking reassurance may also try to self-reassure, repeatedly telling themselves that their fear won't come true.

To your family member with OCD, the reassurance often feels necessary and totally warranted. He believes that once he receives reassurance, he'll be free to move on. And to move on without the reassurance feels too risky. Coping with that risk may lead to some kind of panic attack or anxiety episode, which could be devastating, or at least time consuming. You want him to move on. He wants to move on. So it seems logical that his asking one more time (and your answering one more time) gets everybody what they want…except it's never really just one more time.

Another problem with seeking reassurance is what it does to the logical brain. If you recall from the earlier discussion on avoidance, the brain uses a kind of opposite language. Rather than tell you what to do, it presents explanations for what you've already done. Reassurance is about eliminating doubt. If you attempt to convince yourself of something (even if it's something you believe you already know), and convincing oneself is the behavior of a person who's experiencing doubt, then your brain can only conclude you must be experiencing doubt. So, for example, if a person is suffering with intrusive thoughts about harming others, she may repeatedly reassure herself that she isn't violent and would never wish to cause pain to a loved one. This behavior, however, is the behavior of a person who really isn't sure (at least that's how the brain perceives it). So the more she tries to convince herself, the more she ultimately feels uncertain.

Confessing

Confessing is a form of reassurance-seeking, because it sets up the person receiving the confession to offer reassurance. For example, someone with moral obsessions is concerned that he was dishonest on a questionnaire. As he stews over it, he starts to feel the pressure of thoughts and feelings about being a bad person. He says to you, "I only read the questions one time, so I might have missed something." Automatically the words "That's okay" fall from your lips. Mission accomplished. He now has an assurance from you that if he answered a question dishonestly, it was through no malicious intent.

Let's say your family member is afraid of getting sick from touching a doorknob. Feeling as if she's drowning in thoughts of getting some terminal illness, she casually mentions: "Oh hey, I touched the doorknob on my way in. What's for breakfast?" Maybe you notice the randomness of the comment, maybe not. If you engage her in a discussion about it, you'll ultimately find yourself saying "Don't be silly, you won't get sick." If you say nothing, you'll have still basically said the same thing, because you didn't freak out and say "What?! You touched the doorknob? Quick, let's get you to the hospital!" You can't win. The only way you could come close to sidestepping the confession trap is to comment that you didn't hear what she was saying, but then she might not believe you. Don't be hard on yourself if you find this extremely frustrating.

Sometimes confessing takes the form of simply informing you that a thought is happening. Perhaps your family member who does so is trying to feel "just right" by vocalizing a random thought. Or it may be guilt-driven—your family member feels you have to know that he's thinking some sexual, violent, or otherwise unacceptable thought. Though it may seem like a verbal running faucet of things you don't need to hear, your family member is very likely confessing only what he feels he can't hold back. Consider that this may represent only a tiny percentage of the noise inside his head.

Why Your Family Member May Be Seeking Reassurance

Reassurance-seeking pervades most forms of OCD, with the possible exception of Just Right OCD, which may take a more internal perfectionist approach to seeking certainty, because only the person obsessing can know whether something feels "right." In most other cases, the OCD sufferer seeks input from the outside world (from family members especially) in his quest for certainty.

Common Forms of Reassurance-Seeking and Confessing

(Listed by type of obsessions)

Contamination obsessions

- Asking what has been touched (and when, and by whom)

- Asking for confirmation that various things don't result in illness or other dangers

- Researching contamination issues online (for example, typing "diseases spread through contact" into a search engine)

- Repeatedly asking doctors or other experts about contamination-related dangers

- Confessing that items have been touched or that cleaning/ washing may not have been performed perfectly

Hyper-responsibility (checking) obsessions

- Asking whether light switches, appliances, doors, and locks have been appropriately closed or shut off

- Researching the statistical likelihood of catastrophes resulting from things left unchecked (for example, how many house fires are caused by appliances left on)

- Confessing that items might not have been checked or were only checked a limited number of times

Sexual obsessions

- Asking whether you think he's capable of fitting into a sexual category that he doesn't want to fit into

- Asking opinions of "experts" on sexuality issues, including repeatedly asking for reassurance on online forums devoted to the subject

- Reading "coming out" stories to make sure she doesn't identify with them

- Reading news reports about sex crimes to make sure she doesn't identify with the accused

- Using visual tests to get self-reassurance (for example, watching heterosexual sex scenes to get reassurance that he's aroused by the opposite sex rather than the same sex)

- Confessing the presence of unwanted sexual thoughts

Violent obsessions

- Asking whether you think he'd ever harm anyone

- Asking opinions of "experts" on issues such as sociopathy and "snapping," including repeatedly asking for reassurance on online forums devoted to the subject

- Combing the news for stories about murders, either to make sure she hasn't committed any or to make sure she doesn't identify or share any similarities with the killers

- Confessing the presence of unwanted violent thoughts

Religious obsessions

- Asking whether you think he has committed blasphemy or is performing his religious duties the "right" way

- Repeatedly seeking the advice of religious authorities .

- Rereading religious scripture, to ensure that he's understanding and following it perfectly

- Confessing antireligious or blasphemous thoughts

Moral obsessions

- Asking whether you think she did a bad thing (for example, "Is it cheating if I touched another boy's arm on the dance floor when I was dancing with my boyfriend?")

- Asking whether you'd ever do or ever did what he's obsessing about

- Confessing that he may have acted inappropriately or dishonestly (such as disclosing that he might have peeked at a classmate's test answer but can't remember exactly)

- Confessing the presence of inappropriate or immoral thoughts

Relationship obsessions

- Asking whether you think the relationship is as it should be

- Asking whether you love her or whether you know she loves you

- Confessing unwanted thoughts about the relationship (including thoughts about your appearance, fidelity, and relationship issues in general)

Understanding Reassurance

It would be nice if flat-out denial of all reassurance worked all the time and in every situation. It does work sometimes for some people and is often necessary to crack more extreme commitments to this compulsion. But it depends on your relationship to the person with OCD. If that person is your daughter, for example, consider that as her parent, you've been the authority figure for a long time. You've traditionally had the answers, so it's inevitable that she's going to come to you for reassurance. You reassured her when she was little that nothing under the bed or in the closet was going to get her in the middle of the night. So her expectation that you'll reassure her that there's no bogeyman in her fingernails that will give her a horrible disease if she fails to wash is a pretty reasonable one. If the person in your family with OCD is your husband, consider that he chose you out of all others to be his partner in life—a choice likely made, at least in part, based on the idea that you represent a core set of values and beliefs that he approves of. Your husband is saying you represent a moral ideal to such an extent that you may sleep in his bed, parent his children, and see him unshaven in his underwear. So again, it's not an unreasonable expectation that you're a viable source of information on what's right, good, safe, and so forth. So bearing in mind this special relationship, ask yourself: would it do the relationship more justice for you to (a) give in to your loved one's OCD and give reassurance or (b) help your loved one break the obsessive-compulsive cycle? Often the harder choice is the smarter and the more beneficial one.

Reality Checks

There's a difference between a reality check and compulsive reassurance. Everyone is entitled to a reality check, so long as a reassurance-seeking cycle hasn't already begun. A reality check is an answer to a question. It's not a guarantee, and it doesn't provide certainty. A reality check is always brief—up or down, yes or no—and doesn't include detailed supporting facts. It's simply an answer based on the speaker's reality. If the person asking the question is willing to accept the answer, then it can be useful for moving forward. If the person asking the question doesn't accept the answer, then it becomes a matter of reassurance-seeking and needs to be shut down. For example, if the question is "Can I get HIV from touching a surface that might have had blood on it?" the answer is "No—absolutely not." But does hearing that answer provide certainty? Not really. It's always possible that there's some unknown variable. Maybe there's a rare, undiscovered version of HIV that can be transmitted by touch. The person with Contamination OCD doesn't want to be the case study and may feel compelled to get more reassurance. But still, based on all that we know, the answer is no.

To take it a step further, reality check—is the sky blue? The answer is yes. Does this answer provide certainty? No. First of all, how do you define the sky? Is it the air, the clouds, the stars, the vacuum of space? Second, is the sky *always* blue? Sometimes it's gray, orange, or lavender. And what is blue, anyway? Is it what *I* see and call "blue," or is it what *you* see and call "blue"? Are we seeing the same thing? If this is annoying to read, consider how annoying it would be to experience a similar argument in your own head. So, in order for a reality check to be useful, it has to be accepted. If your family member's OCD is mild to moderate, a reality check is sometimes enough. Let's say your family member with moral obsessions wants to know whether choosing not to give money to a homeless person on the street makes him a bad person. If you believe the answer is no and tell him as much, he may just drop it. But if he follows up with clarifying questions and starts painting you into a corner of having to explain *why* he's not a bad person, that's where we get into reassurance territory.

Identify the Compulsion, Not the Person, as the Problem

Among the sadder things I've seen in my clinical work is the fed-up family member: the mom who can't stand her daughter; the husband who just doesn't like his wife anymore; the son who just thinks his dad is pathetic; the sister who has renamed her sibling "Captain Annoying." Reassurance-seeking can utterly decimate relationships, because it twists and bends family members into a part of the compulsion. Even though you should be careful not to treat your family member with OCD as though she *is* her compulsions, she may be treating *you* as though you're a function of her compulsions! That's not fair, but she isn't doing this to harm you. She really feels as if she can't help it. But by binding you to the reassurance cycle, she dehumanizes you, controls you, and burdens you with the responsibility of keeping her from falling apart. So it's extremely important that you identify reassurance-seeking and confessing as a third party, an unwanted guest in the relationship, by having a conversation that starts with "We need to do something about the reassurance-seeking."

Invite Collaboration

Reassurance leads to one thing only: more requests for reassurance. If the cycle has already begun—if your family member repeatedly asks for reassurance that his fears won't come true—the only way you can help him is by breaking the cycle. The difficulty is that if you unilaterally cut off reassurance after having provided it so many times, you'll cause your family member not only a lot of pain and anxiety, but also anger at the seeming injustice. You, after all, have to take some responsibility for getting your family member strung out on this "drug." Time after time, he asked you for a hit of reassurance, and he felt better, so long as you kept it coming. If you try to cut off his supply, he'll start doing wildly imaginative things to get it. He may find ways to trick you into "giving up the goods" without your even knowing it. Let's say you and your family member with violent obsessions are watching TV when a news flash comes on about a local murder. He says: "Oh, that's awful. Interesting thing, murder. Can't imagine what it must be like to snap and do something crazy like that, y'know?... I'm nothing like that guy, so I just can't figure out how it could happen, y'know?" Then it's either you commenting on how ridiculous he's being (thereby reassuring him) or the sound of crickets.

The only way you can effectively reduce and eventually eliminate your family member's reassurance-seeking is by coming to an agreement ahead of time about how it will be done. This "contract" is instrumental in letting everyone off the hook long enough for things to get back to a healthy place. It begins with you simply asking, "Can we work on this?"

Interrupt the Obsessive-Compulsive Cycle (with Permission)

Make a contract, and put it in writing. Make it specific to the obsession, and make it clear as to why the two of you are working on reducing reassurance-seeking. For example:

> *Because OCD is causing pain to me and my family, I am committing to do what it takes to get better. I am going to put maximum effort into resisting the urge to seek reassurance for my obsession with _____.*
> *I accept that it is my responsibility to accept uncertainty and use my coping skills while I sit with the pain of resisting seeking reassurance.*
>
> *I hereby give permission to _____ [you] to deny me reassurance when I cannot find the strength to resist asking for it. _____ [you] may say the following:*
>
> - *I know you're struggling, but we agreed that I wouldn't answer these types of questions.*
>
> - *I can't answer that.*
>
> - *That's reassurance-seeking, which makes your OCD worse, and I'm not going to do that because I love you.*
>
> - *I can't hear you over your OCD.*

- *We're not talking about that.*

- *Well, that's an interesting thought.*

- *Remember the contract.*

I give _____ [you] permission to decide independently what constitutes reassurance-seeking, and in order to get better, I am willing to accept your assessment of each situation as the right one, even when I disagree.

Consider what other things you could say to your family member when she's asking for reassurance. Carefully negotiate terms with your family member. What might be a good deflection for one person could trigger a greater urge to seek reassurance for another. Among the most important aspects here is that you must be willing to acknowledge that resisting seeking reassurance both requires effort and requires tolerance of pain. If you don't, your family member will perceive your denial of reassurance only as a punishment. Punishments don't produce better behavior—they produce only defiance and manipulation. But also remember that *you* have to tolerate pain to hold fast against the demand for reassurance. If this pain is unbearable, then you need to find a way to relieve it while still resisting accommodating the OCD. This may mean walking out of the room or even leaving the house at times.

The Reassurance Book

If it's too difficult to commit to a contract to eliminate reassurance-seeking, try first removing the verbal aspect of reassurance-seeking. Relegate all reassurance-seeking questions and confessions to the written word. Take a notebook, title it "Reassurance Book," then work with your family member to determine terms for its use. For example, she might be allowed to write five reassurance questions per day, which you'll respond to once a day. Success with the reassurance book hinges on the understanding from the beginning that its purpose is to gradually reduce the number of questions and confessions to zero. If a reassurance book is used indefinitely, it will just become another form of reassurance-seeking.

Other Strategies for Helping a Family Member Reduce Reassurance-Seeking

Once you and your family member have agreed that the problem is OCD, that the compulsion is reassurance-seeking, and that the goal is to reduce it, there are several ways to block or deny reassurance. Just remember that you need to do so with kindness and understanding, not anger and vengefulness. The problem with responding in anger to reassurance-seeking is that your angry tone will nullify the relief your family member is seeking. If he asks you whether "xyz" makes him dirty (or dangerous or a bad person) and you snap, "No!" all he hears is that you're irritated and dismissive and must not really have heard the question or how important it was. He'll just ask again later. So even if you ultimately give in to a request for reassurance, stay calm. Continue to collaborate with your family member on what works and what doesn't. Here are some strategies to consider:

- Silence. Literally don't respond to the question.

- Walk out of the room. As soon as you hear reassurance-seeking, just get out of there!

- Answer a different question—any question you feel like answering.

- Give the opposite of reassurance.

- Pretend you don't speak the same language.

- Repeat the question back.

- Create an impossible barter system, such as requiring fifty push-ups (or dollars) for each question.

- If your family member is in treatment, use the therapist as a scapegoat for your inability to reassure, as in "Your therapist says I can't answer that."

Don't start experimenting on your own. For example, responding with the opposite of reassurance ("Yes, your fear is true!") may be an effective way to block the compulsion, but unless you and your family member have agreed to this strategy, your words will simply sound cruel. Keep the process collaborative. And generally try to preface the outright denial of reassurance with some display of empathy, such as a kind look, a comment about how hard it must be to face the uncertainty, or a simple "I love you."

Cognitive Restructuring and Reassurance

Catching cognitive distortions and challenging them logically can be a powerful tool for resisting compulsions. However, be careful not to unwittingly give reassurance by constantly pointing out why you think your family member's thinking is distorted by the OCD. For example, if your family member with sexual orientation obsessions says to you, "I noticed that guy was attractive, so I must be gay now," don't say, "Noticing another man is attractive doesn't make you gay," even though this seems like a logical point. A better strategy in this case would be to say nothing at all. Maybe shrug. Though it can be useful for your loved one to work on catching and challenging his own distorted thinking, your input will almost always be a part of a reassurance compulsion. By reminding him over and over that his ideas are just OCD ideas, you're basically telling him he's not gay. That means he won't learn to accept uncertainty and will rely more heavily on your input.

Integrate and Model Healthy Behaviors

Work with your family member to come up with a variety of strategies to help him resist this torturous compulsion. Mocking your family member won't help reduce the reassurance-seeking, but humor might. As his reassurance-seeking decreases, fill the void with meaningful conversation. Talk about issues that he and you genuinely connect on. Rebuild the relationship by making communication something to look forward to.

This is also a good time to pay attention to your own desire for reassurance, reassurance that your family member is better or is going to get better. You can't expect him to bite his tongue every time he wants reassurance about his obsession if you keep asking him for reassurance that he's okay. He may be okay; he may not be okay. Talking about it is only going to trigger reassurance-seeking urges in both of you. Model the ability to cope by letting your family member with OCD see you trust in his ability to cope.

Consider This

Resisting reassurance-seeking involves confronting a specific kind of pain. At the time your family member is seeking reassurance, she really believes that the pain of simply sitting with her obsession will never subside. This belief is often reinforced by self-experimentation with resisting. For example, your family member has a question in mind and tells herself she won't ask it because it's a compulsion. But the OCD argues something like "If you don't get an answer, you'll obsess forever." She tries to ignore that thought but several hours later gives in. Then she feels better. But that's not all. Because she tried to resist and "failed," she now has evidence that she cannot survive without the reassurance. So the next time she feels the urge to ask, she will really believe that asking is essential to her survival. Until she gets better, she won't know such beliefs are just OCD trickery.

Your Struggle

When your family member is repeatedly asking you to answer the same questions or to sit and listen to his ridiculous (or disturbing or disgusting) confessions, it's exhausting. It's infuriating. Why doesn't he just shut up about it? In cases like these, spouses see their partners at their ugliest, siblings see each other at their most irritating, and parents may begin to see their children as annoying burdens.

When a family member is seeking reassurance and confessing, you might feel like a slave to your family member's OCD. What do you do—answer her question to shut her up just long enough to get something done until the next question comes around? Or don't answer the question and just tune her out as she begs and pleads for relief from her pain? It's not easy, and it's not all your fault.

Chapter 7

When a Family Member Is Checking

"Let me just check one more time."

"Did you check that? Well, check and be sure."

"Can you check for me?"

"I'm gonna go back and check real quick."

"Check again, to be safe. Better safe than sorry, right?" Wrong. Better sorry than living your life looking over your shoulder.

Checking compulsively means returning to an item or location for the purpose of getting certainty that it remains the way you'd like it to be. We all do some amount of checking. People without OCD sometimes check to make sure they locked the door, turned off the stove, and so on. But when OCD turns checking into a mandate that cannot be disobeyed, and more time is spent checking things than enjoying them in the first place, the results can be torturous. Checking behaviors are among the most frequent form of compulsions, and one way of looking at the function they serve for OCD sufferers is that they reduce the risk of being right about the prediction that negative events will occur. This relieves the pain of accepting uncertainty (Rotge et al. 2008).

Why Your Family Member May Be Checking

Checking comes in many forms. Reassurance-seeking (see the previous chapter) is essentially a form of checking. Your family member is checking to make sure her fear won't come true, and she's using your response as the evidence. In other cases, checking means checking for a certain thought, feeling, or physical sensation. Most commonly, checking comes in the form of returning to a scene in a repetitive manner.

Although most frequently seen in conjunction with, not surprisingly, checking (hyper-responsibility) obsessions, checking often occurs with other obsessions as well.

Common Checking Compulsions

(Listed by type of obsessions)

Hyper-responsibility (checking) obsessions

- Checking light switches
- Checking electrical outlets
- Checking locks
- Checking faucets
- Checking appliances
- Checking doors

- Checking anything that failure to check could result in some unwanted consequence

Contamination obsessions

- Checking to see whether items are contaminated

- Checking to see whether hands or other body parts are clean or dirty

- Checking to see whether people have touched contaminated items or whether they've washed

Just Right obsessions

- Checking to make sure items are lined up perfectly

- Checking to see whether feelings are "right" for a given situation

- Checking to see whether words were articulated or understood perfectly (for example, asking for people to repeat themselves, excessively rewinding/replaying dialogue from TV shows)

Sexual obsessions

- Checking to see whether there has been a "groinal response" to a trigger

- Checking for evidence that an unwanted sexual act has occurred

- Monitoring other people's reactions, to see whether they indicate something about a sexual obsession

- Mentally checking to see whether sexual thoughts are present or whether sexual thoughts are appropriate to the situation

Violent obsessions

- Checking to ensure that potentially dangerous items have been removed or disabled

- Checking people's reactions to ensure they haven't been harmed

- Mentally checking to see whether violent thoughts are present or whether violent thoughts are appropriate to the situation

Relationship obsessions

- Checking for feelings of love or attraction

- Checking to be certain a comment about the relationship was heard or understood

Religious obsessions

- Checking to ensure that no blasphemous behaviors have taken place

- Mentally checking for unwanted antireligious or blasphemous thoughts

Moral obsessions

- Checking clothing tags, ingredients, or other "fine print" issues to ensure no moral beliefs have been violated

- Checking lights, faucets, and appliances to ensure no electricity, water, or other resources are being wasted

- Checking exams, forms, or other written materials to ensure 100 percent honesty

- Mentally checking to ensure that a statement is 100 percent honest

Identify the Compulsion, Not the Person, as the Problem

As with other compulsions, if you haven't already started to accommodate checking, then don't. You can save your family member a lot of pain by cutting him off at the pass the first time around. But given that you're reading this, you've very likely found yourself accommodating checking in a variety of ways, including:

- Allowing extra time for your family member to complete a checking ritual

- Checking on behalf of your family member, to save him or her the trouble

The thing to remember is that you aren't really accommodating the *person*. You're accommodating the *ritual*, the checking. The checking is getting between you and your loved one, between you and being on time, between you and being relaxed. Consider how the checking is getting in your family member's way. Is she missing work, school, or social events? Is he disrupting vacations or other events to go back to check something?

Invite Collaboration

Once the cycle has begun, it has to be unraveled before it can be cut off. What this means is that once you've become an instrumental part of your family member's obsessive-compulsive cycle, you can't just pull the rug out from under her. Doing so would result in an increase in irrational thinking and an increase in ritualized behavior. Just like reducing reassurance-seeking, reducing checking will involve coming to some form of agreement with your family member on how the responsibility of checking or accommodating checking will be gradually shifted away from you, onto her, and then off the planet. Ask her, "How can we solve this checking problem?"

Be clear that you don't mean you should check on her behalf. Instead, perhaps the two of you can agree on a limit to how many times she'll check something, and you can give her a reminder when she's reached it. Or perhaps you can gently redirect her when she asks you to check something. Make it clear that you're asking to be involved *differently*, to be involved in a way that doesn't facilitate compulsions. This is another area where the use of agreed-upon statements or code words might come in handy. If you see her perseverating over whether to go back and check something again (for example, she's frozen on the doorstep, and you know she's thinking about going back in and checking the lights just one more time), can you say something like "spaghetti and meatballs" to snap her out of it?

Interrupt the Obsessive-Compulsive Cycle (with Permission)

Once you've both agreed to collaborate, a good starting point might be determining how long you're willing to wait for your family member to complete a checking ritual before you move on. Then, if you and your family member are leaving the house and he wants to check each light switch, he knows how much time he has to do so. When the time is up, you'll leave, with or without him (as agreed, not in frustration). Each week, work on reducing the time for checking, and then, together, experiment with leaving no time for checking. It may be helpful to create a chart for tracking the gradual reduction of checking.

If you've been roped into checking on behalf of your family member (for example, it's your "job" to check all the locks), then this too will have to be gradually stopped. Although this is one of the easier accommodations to stop making, I still wouldn't recommend stopping all at once. Remember, every time you check for your family member, it may seem as if you're saving both of you time, but in the end you're still negatively reinforcing the idea that checking is necessary and tolerance of uncertainty is not. This will cost you both more time and energy in the long run.

Let's say your family member has an extended ritual for checking the door locks when leaving the house. To save time, you've been volunteering to do additional checks after he has left the house. You might negotiate a plan in which you move from step to step as each becomes better tolerated, such as:

1. Check the locks while he watches you.

2. Check only specifically identified "important" locks while he watches you.

3. Check the locks without him watching you.

4. Don't check the locks, but leave the house for only a short period of time before returning.

5. Don't check the locks, and leave for increasingly longer periods of time.

It's important to monitor your feelings during this process. If she can tell you're irritated, then the process will cease to be an invitation to better health and become a criticism, another source of anxiety, and a reason for your family member to defend her behavior. It's always okay to tell your family member that you can see how hard it is to resist checking. Making that clear will be more productive than conveying how disruptive it is for you to allow her to check.

Integrate and Model Healthy Behaviors

When putting your foot down about checking rituals, keep it short and simple. A long-winded explanation of why something doesn't need to be checked will only function as a form of reassurance and ultimately validate the same thought process that leads to checking in the first place. This doesn't mean you have to be cruel or heartless. You can acknowledge that it's hard for your family member to resist checking and that it comes with a lot of terrifying thoughts of things going terribly wrong. Consider that a family member who compulsively checks locks is trying to neutralize thoughts of things like armed burglars breaking into the house and harming you. Compulsively checking the light switch may be an attempt to neutralize intrusive thoughts of an electrical short setting the house ablaze.

The consequences of some tragedy occurring as a result of failure to check "one more time" appear heartbreaking. But the real heartbreak comes from the fear of being at fault. If you do any excessive checking yourself, or if you're encouraging any excessive checking in your household, scale it back to just below your level of comfort. And as always, use the time saved by not performing rituals to do something meaningful with your family member. Consider what it might mean to your family member if there was time to stop for ice cream on the way to an appointment because you got out of the house more quickly without checking.

Consider This

At the heart of all checking is the fear that failure to check will result in tragedy and the realization that it was easily preventable. To the OCD sufferer, one more check, no matter how burdensome, is such a small and easy thing to do to ensure safety from an obsession. How could your family member cope with the knowledge that if he had checked one more time, the house might not have burned down or a loved one might not have been harmed? Now that he's working on getting better, everyone is telling him not to check, that checking is bad. But what if? What if something happens? Imagine what it must feel like to resist compulsive checking when you have a movie playing over and over in your head of tragedy after tragedy occurring and people—mostly loved ones—blaming you for not checking.

Your Struggle

It's so unbelievably disrupting and annoying, isn't it? How many events have you been late for because your family member needed to check something? How many times have you had a movie, a trip to the mall, or a vacation ruined because your family member simply couldn't stop perseverating on what might be going on at home? How many times have you been talking to your family member only to realize that while she's nodding and smiling, she's completely ignoring you, devoting her mental energies to checking for thoughts and feelings instead? You tell her to drop it. It doesn't work. You tell her, "Come on, let's go," but even when she leaves the physical checking behind, the mental checking continues. OCD wins again and again. But you can help your family member do exposure to her fear of uncertainty, and you can help her put the OCD in its place.

Chapter 8

When a Family Member Is Washing and Cleaning

Washing and cleaning may be the easiest compulsions to identify, partly because of the ever-dwindling supply of soap, towels, and cleaning products in the home. Ritualized washing and cleaning can take up a lot of valuable time, and create a tremendous disruption in family functioning on a variety of levels. For one, the family member who's washing or cleaning excessively is failing to do many other important things in life, like get to work on time, not to mention things like just watching TV curled up on the couch with a bowl of popcorn, playing on the floor with the children, or simply relaxing with a cup of tea or reading a book.

Why Your Family Member May Be Washing and Cleaning

Part of what makes washing and cleaning compulsions so tragic has to do with the delicate nature of trying to maintain a sense of certainty throughout any OCD ritual. It's just too easy to perceive recontamination, which necessitates starting the washing or cleaning over again. To illustrate this, consider the process of going to the bathroom. Here are the thoughts an OCD sufferer might have to contend with at each step of the process:

1. Enter bathroom. *I might have touched the door—I had better wash first.*

2. Undo pants. *I touched my belt and my pants—I had better wash.*

3. Sit on toilet and do business. *Make sure I eliminate everything so I don't have to come back soon.*

4. Wipe. *I have to make sure I've wiped every possible molecule of waste from my body—I had better use more paper.*

5. Pull up pants. *I touched my belt again; now my belt is dirtier.*

6. Flush. *I definitely have to wash now.*

7. Touch the faucet handle to turn the water on. *Oh no, I should've used a paper towel or something—I just contaminated the faucet.*

8. Wash. *I have to make sure I wash perfectly, to eliminate all possible contaminants.*

9. Turn off the faucet. *Oh no, I touched the faucet again—the dirty faucet—right after washing. I had better wash again.*

10. Dry hands on hand towel. *Other people use this hand towel, and they don't wash as thoroughly as I do, so now my hands are contaminated again. I had better wash again.*

I could go on, but imagine how your loved one may be getting caught in such a loop. He gets contaminated, then clean, but then often gets contaminated while washing, creating an urge to wash again, and so on and so forth.

Washing and cleaning compulsions are most visible in basic Contamination OCD. However, the very ritual of washing goes beyond simply removing dirt and germs. It has roots in religious practice and in the symbolism of "getting clean" or starting over. As such, it can become a neutralizing tool for many different obsessions. Similarly, cleaning represents getting things right, putting your life in order. You probably have had the experience at least once of finishing a big cleanup of your home or office, looking around and seeing everything exactly as it "should" be, and breathing a big sigh of relief. OCD sufferers have difficulty accepting things as they are in such moments, often setting their sights on the next big sigh of relief.

Common Washing and Cleaning Compulsions

(Listed by type of obsessions)

Contamination obsessions

- Excessive washing and cleaning of hands, body, personal items (for example, phone and keys), and surfaces (in the home, office, or car) to neutralize fear of germs, bodily fluids, or chemicals

Just Right obsessions

- Washing or cleaning to make something look perfectly clean or organized
- Washing or cleaning until a specific "feeling" is achieved

Sexual obsessions

- Excessive washing in an attempt to remove any possible semen or vaginal secretions that could be considered as causing a sexual act if spread to other people

- Washing to represent the neutralization of thoughts (washing away bad thoughts)

Violent obsessions

- Excessive washing to ensure that no dangerous chemicals or deadly germs are spread to other people

- Locking up anything that might be used as a weapon (for example, hammers, knives)

- Hiding chemical cleaning products and other harmful substances

- Washing to represent the neutralization of thoughts (washing away bad thoughts)

Religious obsessions

- Washing after sexual activity, to feel "pure" again

Moral obsessions

- Cleaning to ensure that nobody is put off by things being unclean

Identify the Compulsion, Not the Person, as the Problem

Compulsive washers and cleaners typically put a lot of pressure on their family members to be careful. This leads their family members to walk on eggshells, hoping not to touch the wrong thing and send their loved one into another compulsive fit. It's not fair, and it's okay to be irritated by your family member's demands that you jump through hoops to keep her from having to do more compulsions.

Just never lose sight of the fact that your loved one is not the enemy. OCD is the enemy. It's the OCD that's getting in the way, driving your loved one to attempt to control unwanted thoughts and feelings with washing and cleaning. Washing compulsions are also prolonged by the presence of guilt, despite the fact that washing doesn't seem to actually relieve guilt (Cougle et al. 2012).

Invite Collaboration

Let your family member with OCD know what the problem is—not in a critical way but in an observant, mindful way. Express concern: "I'm worried about how much time you're spending in the bathroom" or "I've noticed you're going through a lot of toilet paper. Is everything okay?" Invite your family member to work with you to address the problem.

As with accommodating any kind of compulsion, the best strategy is to not start accommodating in the first place. But if you've been roped into the cycle, work with your family member to gradually get out of it. Ask how you can help reduce specific problem behaviors: "How can I help you get a handle on your shower time?" "How can we work on cutting down on the hand-washing?" Simply asking whether you can help in general terms is likely to result in requests that you not touch anything and buy more hand sanitizer. The key is to ask whether you can help differently.

Interrupt the Obsessive-Compulsive Cycle (with Permission)

Any time your family member is deeply immersed in a washing or cleaning ritual, you have to be careful when and how you interrupt him. Often an interruption will result in a powerful urge to start the ritual from scratch. Consider what this means for someone whose ritual takes hours. The resulting desperation can lead to anger and then you and your family member will be fighting with each other instead of fighting against the OCD. That's why it's essential to identify the compulsion as the problem and invite collaboration before you intervene.

Once you and your family member are working as a team, there are many ways you can effectively interrupt a washing or cleaning ritual. One way is to point out that your family member is doing a ritual—not in a "Gotcha!" way, but more as a gentle reminder. Use a code word if your family member prefers. Another way is to distract your family member with something else for her to do. Another strategy is to agree to time limits on washing and cleaning and enforce them (this can include shutting off the water when needed or doling out specific amounts of soap). You can reduce the amount of time your family member spends washing and cleaning in general if you, with permission, remove or limit the availability of soap or other items used for washing or cleaning.

Your family member's washing and cleaning compulsions may come with demands that *you* also wash or clean a certain way. You may be accommodating his obsessions by showering after coming home from work, by avoiding touching items that he has cleaned, or by washing your hands in a specific way he prefers. Though it's not advisable to try to trigger your family member's OCD for no reason, it's important that you target and eliminate anything you're doing to "protect" him from anxiety. He'll probably either pull at your heartstrings, begging you to follow through so as not to trigger his OCD, or simply demand that you obey his rules. In either case, you need to establish openly what you'll continue doing on his behalf and for how long, with the goal of gradually eliminating your participation in any washing or cleaning rituals. The endgame is to have you living your own life free from

OCD, enabling you to model healthy behavior so that he can pursue the same goal.

Integrate and Model Healthy Behaviors

As your family member works on reducing compulsions with your support, start integrating your own healthy washing and cleaning habits and enlist her help. This will probably mean you too have to do some exposure in order to model appropriate behavior. Wash your hands only after using the toilet or before a meal. Leave some things messy or dusty in your home. Wear shoes in the house.

As is true for other compulsions, reducing washing and cleaning frees up time. As your family member washes and cleans less, encourage her to engage in activities that are meaningful to her. And the less you have to help her rein in the washing and cleaning, the more time you can spend doing things that matter to *you*.

Consider This

Your family member who is washing and cleaning feels dirty, disgusting, irresponsible, shameful, and charged with the impossible task of guaranteeing that he has removed that which offends him. Whether that's germs, bodily fluids, dust, or bad thoughts, he feels as if he's constantly faced with a choice between doing something he feels control over and accepting a life filled with pain. The situation gets progressively worse, until the controlled behavior becomes out of control—the skin on his hands begins to tear, or the time he spends in the shower begins to overtake the time he spends doing anything else. Now it's a decision between the impossible to achieve and the seemingly impossible to accept. Reality is out of reach, and no matter how much your family member loves and respects you, your voice of reason is just not as loud as OCD's voice of condemnation.

When a Family Member Has OCD

Your Struggle

Living with a compulsive washer or cleaner drains your resources, literally and figuratively. It costs you in terms of cleaning products and increases your utility bills. It costs you in terms of time—it takes you longer to get out of the house, you have to pause the TV show or movie every time she gets up to wash, and you have to wait while she debates whether it's safe to go out to eat. Worst of all, it costs you in terms of respect for your loved one. Watching someone repeatedly engage in a behavior you know is unnecessary, one that's causing her so many problems, one that seems so easy to just stop, chips away at everything she means to you. You suffer too. You suffer the loss of a family member to OCD. You can help get your family member back, but there are no guarantees and the stakes are high. Remember to be kind to yourself.

Chapter 9

When a Family Member Is Doing Mental Rituals

Of all the areas in which being a family member of an OCD sufferer is frustrating, nothing competes with mental rituals (mental compulsions). Remember, a compulsion is something you do in response to an unwanted thought to reduce your discomfort, neutralize the thought, or get a sense of certainty that a fear won't come true. Physical compulsions, such as washing one's hands or checking the stove, are easy to recognize and thus address, but mental compulsions are inherently impossible to observe. It was once imagined that some people simply obsessed for no reason, that they played no active role in an obsessive-compulsive cycle but unwanted thoughts still rained down on them. This prompted the use of terms like "Pure Obsessional" or "pure O" in the mental health world. This view has since been dismissed as inaccurate; those who were previously thought to be obsessing without compulsions were in fact engaging in various forms of self-reassurance and mental rituals (Williams et al. 2011). A study at Rogers Memorial Hospital assessed 1,086 individuals admitted to their program for OCD treatment and identified the existence of obsessions *and* compulsions in all cases, including those in which the patients did not believe or understand that they were doing (Leonard and Riemann 2012).

How Mental Rituals Work

The term "pure O" remains in the lexicon of OCD, mostly as a way for OCD sufferers to identify themselves and each other as neither "checkers" or "washers." This is a good thing in the sense that it reduces the pain of isolation and fosters a sense of community, but it overlooks the fact that checkers and washers engage in physical compulsions only because their mental compulsions are not effective enough.

Consider how much a person might debate with himself whether his hands are clean after touching something like a TV remote. He doesn't want to get up off the couch and engage in a long and painful washing ritual. He could mentally reassure himself that his hands are clean. He could try to think clean thoughts, try to lock out unclean thoughts. He could mentally retrace the steps of each person who might have touched the remote before him, to determine whether they were clean when they touched it. He could imagine a protective coating separating his body from germs. He could mentally chant "I will not get sick if I touch the remote and don't wash." All of these are mental compulsions. Or he could give up trying to resist, get up, and wash.

Why Your Family Member May Be Engaging in Mental Rituals

Every form of OCD involves some amount of mental ritual. From the very moment an unwanted thought presents itself, there's an inner voice that says, *This thought is unwanted and should not be here.* That voice is the seed of the first mental ritual—the first attempt to neutralize, block out, or disprove the content of the unwanted thought. Your family member with OCD may rely on mental rituals as a function of his personality: he may reason, *I'm just an analytical, intellectual sort of person.* Or he may be more intentional or selective in his mental rituals, trying to get his needs for reassurance met without getting "caught" by anyone.

Common Mental Rituals

(Listed by type of obsessions)

Contamination obsessions

- Mentally reviewing or retracing how items might have become contaminated

- Neutralizing unwanted thoughts with "clean" thoughts

- Counting while washing or cleaning, to get a sense of certainty that the washing or cleaning was completed

- Self-reassuring with mental statements like *I know I'm clean* or *I won't get sick*

- Mentally reviewing the potential consequences of being contaminated and whether those consequences can be tolerated

Hyper-responsibility (checking) obsessions

- Retracing the steps involved in checking an item, to feel certain the memory of checking it is accurate

- Mental checking—conjuring up a checked item mentally to see whether it still feels checked (locked, turned off, and so on)

- Self-reassuring with mental statements like *I know the door is locked*

- Counting while checking, to feel certain that the checking was completed

- Mentally reviewing the potential consequences of failing to check and whether those consequences can be tolerated

Just Right obsessions

- Mentally checking to see whether a memory of an object, thought, or feeling is exactly as it "should" be

- Mentally chanting or repeating statements until they feel "right"

Violent obsessions

- Mentally reviewing/analyzing whether violent thoughts could mean something or lead to violent actions

- Mentally checking feelings or bodily sensations for evidence of harm (for example, *Did my hand get a strange feeling when it was near that knife?*)

- Thought neutralizing—replacing thoughts of harm with "safe" thoughts

- Compulsively praying that fears of violent behavior won't come true

- Counting, or indirect mental rituals (for example, *If I say this word four times, it will keep my mother from being harmed*)

- Self-reassuring statements or chants (for example, *I know I'd never harm my son*)

- Mentally reviewing hypothetical scenarios to determine whether he might ever act on violent thoughts

- Compulsive flooding—purposely dwelling on unwanted harm thoughts in an attempt to prove that they're still offensive and won't be acted on

Sexual obsessions

- Mentally reviewing and debating sexual orientation

- Mentally reviewing other people's behavior and statements regarding sexual subjects

When a Family Member Has OCD

- Mentally checking groinal sensations or feelings and emotions connected to erotic arousal
- Thought neutralization—replacing unwanted sexual thoughts with wanted ones
- Compulsively praying that sexual fears won't come true
- Self-reassuring statements or chants (*I'm not attracted to...*)
- Mentally reviewing hypothetical scenarios to determine whether she might ever act on unwanted sexual thoughts
- Compulsive flooding—purposely dwelling on unwanted sexual thoughts in an attempt to prove that they're still offensive and won't be acted on

Relationship obsessions

- Mentally reviewing the quality of the relationship
- Mentally checking for feelings of love or attraction to you
- Mentally reviewing interactions with you that might mean something about the relationship
- Mentally reviewing your past
- Reassuring himself about the relationship

Religious obsessions

- Compulsively praying
- Mentally reviewing religious concepts
- Mentally checking feelings during religiously themed events
- Reassuring herself about her connection to her faith

Moral obsessions

- Mentally reviewing his moral beliefs

- Mentally reviewing his actions and whether those actions were moral

- Mentally reviewing hypothetical situations where morality would be an issue (for example, *If my coworker came on to me, would I cheat on my wife?*)

- Mentally reviewing his conversations to determine whether he might have said anything dishonest or otherwise immoral

Managing Mental Rituals

As a support person for your loved one, the first thing you may need to address is your own struggle with acceptance. In other words, you have to realize you cannot stop your family member from doing compulsions. You might physically block him from washing, but he'll find a way around it if he's desperate enough. If he can't figure out a way to do his physical compulsions, he'll resort to increasing his mental compulsions. And you cannot stop him from doing mental compulsions. That being said, you *can* help him fight his OCD, and you can bolster him with support and encouragement to win the fight.

Identify the Compulsion, Not the Person, as the Problem

You might notice that your family member with OCD is "in her head" a lot. She doesn't seem to listen when you talk. She doesn't seem to be "with it," "together," or "on her game," or she acts distant or aloof. Consider that at such times she may be ritualizing furiously in silence, unable to focus on what's going on around her because she's working really, really hard to complete a mental ritual. Any time you notice she seems to not be paying attention and ask her whether she's doing a ritual, however, don't be surprised if she denies it. It's hard for an OCD sufferer to come to terms with the fact that she's stuck in a loop and is voluntarily engaging in mental behavior that she knows is making it worse. She may say, "I'm just trying to figure something out," and may even resist identifying this as a compulsive behavior. In that case, instead of approaching your loved one from a critical standpoint, let her know that you're concerned, that you can tell she has a lot on her mind, and that it must be really difficult.

Invite Collaboration

Breaking down mental rituals is a dance of getting in the way of the completion of rituals without getting in the way of the presence of unwanted thoughts. If your family member wants your help, distraction is a good strategy. Ask your family member in advance for permission to try to redirect his attention whenever you notice that he's ritualizing. Logic, on the other hand—tempting though it may be to try to help your family member solve the mental quandary he's stuck in—is not a good strategy. If your family member is obsessed with the possibility of being gay, it may seem easy to tell him: "Look, you're not gay. If you were gay, we'd all know, and if we all knew, we'd be okay with it, so just let it go." But the truth is, you can never eliminate all doubt from the mind of a person with OCD. Your attempt to apply logic will only make him feel foolish and ashamed. Ironically, discussing the content of the obsession and trying to come up with a reasonable way of resolving it encourages more compulsive behavior.

Although in reality we all have the freedom to move on from upsetting thoughts at any time, your family member with OCD believes he needs to *do* something before he can move on. You don't want to have any part in reinforcing this false belief. You just want to be a part of the moving on. So invite him to work with you on strategies for walking away from uncertainty, not figuring it out.

Interrupt the Obsessive-Compulsive Cycle (with Permission)

Once your family member has agreed to let you interfere in her mental rituals, consider your relationship to her and use it to your advantage. Let's say you notice that your daughter seems to be engrossed in some kind of conversation in her head. Simply saying, "Honey, can you come here and help me with the dishes, please?" can dislodge her from the loop and give her an opportunity to focus on something else. If it's your partner who has OCD, you might be able to defuse anxieties with some fun or some good-natured teasing. A husband may notice his wife perseverating about something and, with permission, lightly poke her in the arm and say, "Hey, you, cut it out—come back to Earth!" It doesn't always work, but quite often, because rituals are so painful and exhausting, your family member is hoping for permission to stop. She may not be equipped to give herself permission, but your interrupting her gives her a shot at trying.

The biggest accommodations you've made for your family member's mental rituals are in terms of your time. You've probably often felt as if you were being put on pause while he went and completed some task in his head, and then you got unpaused and were expected to resume normal behavior. He may have often asked you to wait for him to finish ritualizing. He may have wanted you to wait to speak, wait to leave, or wait to complete some task. Once you have permission to fight this disorder together with your loved one, you'll need to agree on how much waiting you'll do going forward. If *you* wait less, *he's* more likely to ritualize less.

When it comes to cognitive restructuring, challenging distorted thinking without engaging in compulsive analysis is a delicate procedure you shouldn't attempt to help your loved one with. Let him work on that with his therapist or his workbook. If you participate in attempts to rationalize distorted thinking, you'll likely find yourself facilitating mental rituals. So if your family member starts to explain a mental process to you in great detail and it sounds as if he's trying to resolve his obsession, don't take the bait. Remaining unimpressed with and nonresponsive to his mental rituals will be more effective than trying to keep up with their twists and turns.

Mindfulness Tip

Your family member probably thinks you can't tell when she's doing mental rituals, but you can. You can see it in her eyes, for example. Notice what happens to you when you become aware that your family member is ritualizing. Do you get angry? Do you experience thoughts of how you wish she were different? Do you feel abandoned, as though she's choosing her OCD over you? Rather than trying to shut out these experiences, try to simply observe them. Let them pass. Tell yourself: This is just what's happening now, in this moment. The next moment will eventually arrive.

Integrate and Model Healthy Behaviors

Consider your left elbow. If you're like most people, your left elbow is just another part of your body. You don't try to avoid thinking about your left elbow, but neither do you try to bring up the subject of your left elbow. It just is what it is. If you treat your own obsessive thoughts like your left elbow—as the normal, uninteresting things they are—it will help your loved one address them the same way. Too often, family members unnecessarily upset their loved ones with OCD by asking how they're doing with the obsession. "Is it okay now?" "Are you still worrying about that?" "How's that thing going?" Just as often, family members tiptoe around subject matter that may trigger their loved one's OCD. This is even worse! It only ends up making the subject matter seem more important. Your family member knows that triggers exist in the environment. A TV commercial can easily trigger a violent, sexual, religious, or moral obsession, and having you leap across the coffee table to change the channel will just make your family member feel worse about it. So if you want to help your loved one reduce mental rituals, demonstrate your own ability to let ideas come and go without overreacting.

Consider This

Throughout this book, I've discussed how OCD rituals are intended to foster a sense of certainty. To the OCD sufferer, failure to achieve certainty can equate to failure to be a person of intrinsic value. How can I believe I have self-worth if I can't even believe 100 percent that I won't murder my children, won't contract a terminal illness, or will continue loving my spouse? But people see me doing these compulsions and think I'm nuts. It follows, then, that if I'm going to be a worthwhile individual, I have to figure out a way to disprove my obsessions in silence. This is the isolated world of the "pure O" mental ritualizer. Further, because the rituals are covert, the most sadistic of obsessions creeps in—the fear that it's not even OCD in the first place! So the OCD sufferer who engages primarily in mental compulsions feels isolated from society in general, as someone struggling with mental illness, but also feels isolated from the mental health community, as a person who may not even have the illness.

When a Family Member Has OCD

Give Yourself a Break

It's okay to feel helpless. Sure, you can express heartfelt sympathy—empathy even—for your loved one who's stuck in a cycle of intrusive thoughts and mental rituals. Everyone knows, to some degree, what it's like to go over and over something in your head and not be able to "shut it off." But in the end, identifying and resisting mental rituals is up to your family member. The only way you can help is by supporting her efforts to help herself, and the only way you can remain supportive is by taking care of yourself. So treat yourself well. Don't put everything else that matters to you aside for one person, even one who matters so much to you. She needs you present, waiting for her to return when she escapes the influence of her OCD.

So Now You Know

You did it! You made it through part 2 and hopefully learned a lot about helping and supporting your family member with OCD. So now what? How do you make sense of it all? Don't beat yourself up if you still feel as if you only "sort of" get how you can help. In the next two chapters, I discuss some interesting perspectives of different family members, as well as specific mindfulness and cognitive behavioral tools for use in different types of family relationships. Then I go over how to find good professional help and what treatment may look like, as well as tips and tools for keeping your OCD family strong.

Part 3

Perspectives

In these final two chapters, I discuss more specific issues related to each of the primary relationships within the family system: spousal, parent-child (including parent-teen and parent-adult), sibling, and child-parent. I also go over the complex and sometimes confusing relationship between your family and the variety of treatment providers your family may encounter when seeking help for OCD. You can skip directly to the sections that seem to apply to you the most, but I suggest finding time to read the sections that apply to other members of your family as well. If you're reading this book to better understand your son with OCD, for example, it will be helpful for you to also understand what his sister is going through. Any change in one part of the family system will bring about change in the other parts. The more you know, the more prepared you can be. As your loved one with OCD works toward better mental health, it will be easier for him to maintain those gains if he's rejoining a stable family system.

Chapter 10

OCD and Different Family Dynamics

For the OCD sufferer, whether her obsession is common or relatively unheard of, there's always a sense that *her* problem is the worst problem. In group therapy sessions for OCD sufferers, this phenomenon of "Oh, I *wish* I had your problem" frequently comes up. A Contamination OCD sufferer who jokes that he wishes he had Harm OCD does so for two reasons: his pain is so great it seems no one else's could be as bad, and, anyway, who could really take that "other" obsession seriously? This concept of each individual rising to the peak of her own level of suffering replicates itself throughout the OCD family. In other words, it's not unique to the family member with OCD. For example, Mom can't bear to see her daughter struggle with OCD. But Mom has no idea what it's like to be the *other* kid in the family, dealing with his sister and her OCD. So everyone navigates the maze of the OCD family thinking that his own journey is the hardest. And the kicker is, they're all right. Individuals rise to a level of suffering, and the entire family follows suit.

Throughout this chapter, you'll find lists of obsessions and compulsions that can affect each type of relationship. These lists aren't all-inclusive—I don't mean to suggest that the symptoms listed are the only ones that can affect the relationship. Regarding the lists of dos and don'ts, an important general guideline has to do with how you *invite* your loved one to collaborate with you in addressing the problem. If you recall, once you've identified the compulsive behavior as problematic, the next step is to make it known that you're willing to help. Having read this book, and possibly other articles and books on OCD (like those in the resources), you might feel a strong urge to teach your loved one what you've learned. Here's where it gets tricky: You have to invite collaboration, not ambush him or pressure him with constant lectures on OCD. If you follow your loved one around the house, reading aloud from OCD workbooks, you'll do more harm than good. Your family member's likely response will be to shut down, protect the OCD, and categorically reject your demands that he see the light.

You can't force someone to accept your support, and you can't be your family member's therapist. The position of supportive family member is an unenviable one at times. Once you make it known that you're available and want to help, you may have to wait, observe, and just try not to make matters worse by overly accommodating the compulsions. This waiting requires great strength and patience, but trying to *command* your loved one to get better will take you out of the role of supportive family member, and that's where you're needed.

General Dos and Don'ts for Supporting Your Family Member with OCD

Do	Don't
Express a desire to understand your family member's OCD, and educate yourself about OCD by reading books on the subject.	Attribute your family member's OCD behaviors to a character or personality flaw.

Encourage cognitive-behavioral treatment and psychiatric evaluation in a nonjudgmental way.	Personalize your family member's struggles, or make your family member's anxiety about you.
Seek support and treatment for yourself where warranted, including individual therapy and support groups for families of OCD sufferers (online, or in person if available).	Criticize or mock your family member's symptoms (particularly in front of other family members) or speak disparagingly of your family member's OCD in public.
Praise or express gratitude for overall efforts to improve.	Use OCD as an insult, or say "Don't be so OCD about that."
Find humor *with* your family member about the OCD.	Go out of your way to point out steps not yet taken or slip-ups.
Practice mindfulness and patience in stressful situations.	Act as though you're your family member's therapist or educator, or take sole responsibility for your family member's mental health.
Express empathy while withholding reassurance.	Blame yourself or other family members for the existence of the OCD.
Reinforce exposure work as relevant to your family member's therapy assignments.	Accommodate rituals, offer reassurance, or assume responsibilities for your family member to facilitate avoidance.

When Your Partner Has OCD

Ah, love. It's all roses and butterflies, isn't it? And work. You met a person; that person became *the* person, *your* person; and then somehow you both ended up as an entity greater than the sum of its parts. Whether you have kids or not, you're a family. You're a committed couple, and there's something really amazing about that. When you decide after some amount of time around this other person that you genuinely care as much about his happiness as your own (well, almost as much, anyway), it's a strange and wonderful feeling. This other person becomes something between a partner in crime and a third arm to scratch your head while you try to solve crimes. If this other person is happy, that actually *means* something, and not just because the person will be nicer to you or credit you with her happiness. No, it just means something to you that the person—your person—is happy.

When you're married to or in a committed relationship with someone who has OCD, you aren't married or committed to that person's OCD. It may feel as though you are, but that's actually a product of your own distorted thinking. It's a magnification, or at least a simplification, of what's really going on. Your partner's OCD is like that ugly couch he brought with him when you moved in together. It's not without its charm, but it's not something that adds value to your home. But the couch is not your partner.

Common Compulsions That Might Affect Your Partner's Relationship with You

(Listed by type of obsessions)

Sexual obsessions

- Avoiding intimacy as an attempt to avoid unwanted sexual thoughts

- Engaging in excessive sexual behavior as a form of reassurance

- Seeking reassurance about your belief in his sexual orientation

Harm obsessions

- Avoiding closeness for fear of harming you
- Seeking reassurance about your belief that he won't harm you

Hyper-responsibility (checking) obsessions

- Demanding that his time or your time be spent checking items
- Avoiding or ending joint ventures (for example, vacations) to perform checking rituals

Contamination obsessions

- Avoiding contact with bodily fluids (yours or hers)
- Avoiding contaminating you or being contaminated by you
- Requesting that you engage in specific decontamination or avoidance rituals
- Avoiding shared responsibilities at home that may involve contamination (for example, taking out the trash)

Relationship obsessions

- Avoiding you altogether, or avoiding activities that high-light the fact that you're a couple (date nights, vacations, and so on)
- Seeking reassurance about the stability of the relationship

- Compulsively confessing thoughts about the relationship (including confessing finding others attractive or finding flaws in you)

Moral obsessions

- Excessive reassurance-seeking or confessing about perceived moral missteps

Intimacy

Intimacy means being so connected to another person, so close, that your mind and body may touch at the same time. It doesn't always include physical contact, but it does require some form of closeness. A person can provide the *illusion* of intimacy—have a conversation, engage in sexual activity, give a compliment, even express genuine love—all while mentally attending to other things, such as obsessing and engaging in mental rituals, but true intimacy requires paying full attention to the other person. This is hard (but not impossible) for OCD sufferers. Even in intimate moments, to choose not to acknowledge obsessive thoughts and urges to do compulsions feels like choosing to ignore a fire alarm. That creates a sense of "going through the motions," or a sense of potentially being in denial of important warning signs. People do this every day, but OCD sufferers are more aware of it.

During intimate moments, your partner with OCD may often feel like an actor *playing the part* of a person being intimate, hoping not to get caught doing the "real" task of remembering lines, swinging a mental bat wildly to keep unwanted thoughts away. This is especially true in sexual intimacy. Aksaray et al. (2001) found that women with OCD, for example, were more likely to be nonsensual, anorgasmic, and avoidant and to experience significant dissatisfaction with sexual interactions compared to women with generalized anxiety disorder. This was particularly evident in those with contamination obsessions or fears related to bodily secretions. Men are likely equally affected.

Consider that if you're overly critical of your partner, he won't feel safe opening up to you, so it's unfair to expect him to take the risk of leaving his unwanted thoughts and rituals behind. He needs to know that no matter what happens, you won't be a source of shame. Or consider that your partner may be having unwanted thoughts about being gay, about harming you, about harming the children, or about getting or spreading disease, and he's torn between meeting your completely rational emotional need for closeness and accepting that any of these things may be true. Abbey, Clopton, and Humphreys (2007, 1188) found that "individuals with more severe obsessional thinking may be preoccupied with their intrusive thoughts to the extent that they have less time and less mental energy to devote to being intimate with their love partners." In other words, the disorder drains the resources necessary for tending to the relationship. It's essential that you not confuse your partner's being "in his head a lot" with disinterest in you. If you pressure your partner to prove he wants to be with you, you stop being a safe place to return to. Then he's stuck between his disorder and your rejection. He may appear to be "in his head" to escape from reality, but more likely he's trying to escape from his head, trying to get back to you.

Triangulation

The natural response to anxiety is to seek relief. Anxiety exists within the individual, but it can also exist within a couple or the larger system of the family. In the 1960s, a therapist by the name of Murray Bowen developed a concept in psychodynamic family therapy called *triangulation* (Charles 2001): When anxiety exists in a relationship, one person (usually the more emotionally reactive person, according to Bowen) will pull a third party into the equation, to ease the anxiety and stabilize the relationship. If a husband and wife are in conflict, for example, the wife may turn to one of the children for emotional support. This somewhat eases the strain on the marriage but at the expense of the child's emotional development, which is stalled by the child's using his emotional resources to care for the parent. When the child grows up, anxiety in *his* marriage will likely result in triangulation of someone from the next generation, and this pattern may be repeated each generation until someone gets treatment and learns to improve his or her ability to separate thoughts and feelings.

Most books on OCD don't discuss concepts in psychodynamic therapy, because there's little evidence that psychodynamic approaches are effective for OCD (Foa 2010). However, I mention triangulation here because it seems to happen in a lot of OCD families. If your partner has OCD, her anxiety creates anxiety in the relationship. It's not healthy to ignore this relationship anxiety, but it's worse to bring your children into your strategy for coping with your partner's OCD or managing your anxiety in general. It won't help your partner, it won't help you in the long run, and it has the potential to harm the children and even future generations.

This doesn't mean you should keep your partner's OCD a secret from the children. To the contrary, educate them in a way that helps them understand that your partner's behavior is not their fault (see "When Your Parent Has OCD," later in this chapter). If you and your partner are working on the OCD, praise your partner's efforts when appropriate. Let it be known that your children come from parents who overcome adversity.

Accommodations

Adults rely heavily on their romantic relationships for support, and in your desire to "help" reduce your partner's anxiety, you may find yourself accommodating her symptoms, which interferes in treatment and causes symptoms to worsen (Boeding et al. 2013).

Your partner's OCD may have tricked her into using you as a function of the disorder. You may be on the receiving end of ridiculous demands to check the lights one more time, shower before you touch your partner, leave your items at the door to avoid contaminating the house, do all the chores that trigger anxiety, respond to the same (often offensive and upsetting) questions and confessions over and over, and more. You may feel as though you've stopped being a partner and become an employee—more like an indentured servant, really. The toll this can take on a relationship knows no bounds. Once you stop communicating on a person-to-person level, everything can fall apart. For this reason, you must try to help your partner by reducing your accommodation.

Coping with a partner who has OCD can seem like a double bind. If your partner is willing to work on the OCD, and you're resisting accommodating her compulsions, it will create stress in the relationship. Your partner may get angry at you for denying her the reassurance she craves. She may feel incapable of touching you because you refuse to change your clothes after going outside the house. You'll have to contain the stress she emanates while she works on the OCD, without giving in to her demands for compulsive accommodation. But you're not allowed to contribute to the conflict by criticizing her or expressing anger toward her for not getting better fast enough. It isn't fair (for either of you). But then who said OCD plays fair?

So, in the end, you have to find healthy ways to cope with this stress, ways of coping that won't undo the progress you and your partner are trying to make with the OCD. This may mean giving yourself time-outs, exercising, engaging in a mindful meditation practice, seeking the support of your friends, seeking psychotherapy for yourself, or all of the above. You have to remember that if your partner gets better, it'll be because *she* did the work. But you have to also remember that if she did the work, it's because *you* helped create an environment where that was possible. Creating this environment, where your partner won't be afraid to disclose her symptoms and will be willing to do the work, is key.

Dos and Don'ts for Supporting Your Partner with OCD

Do	Don't
Express a desire to understand your partner's OCD but a willingness to accept that you may not fully understand it.	Attribute your partner's OCD behaviors to a character or personality flaw, or use your partner's OCD as a weapon when in conflict.
Encourage your partner to get cognitive behavioral treatment and psychiatric evaluation in a nonjudgmental way.	Use shame or threats (for example, threats of divorce) to pressure your partner to get treatment.
Find humor with your partner about the OCD. Use your own private language to keep it light when possible.	Criticize or mock your partner's symptoms (particularly in front of your children).
Be patient and nonjudgmental where intimacy is concerned.	Use shame and criticism to address sexual problems that may be related to OCD.

When Your Young Child Has OCD

Children who develop OCD before the age of ten may be more likely than adults with OCD to engage in repeating and ordering compulsions and to also have tics (sudden and involuntary vocal or motor spasms), but fortunately their OCD is no less likely to respond to cognitive-behavioral treatment (Nakatani et al. 2011). Early attention to symptoms and seeking professional help to get adequate treatment for your child with OCD is important, because when he becomes an adult, he may be unlikely to seek treatment (Stengler et al. 2013), possibly because he'll simply have grown used to his symptoms.

OCD can be diagnosed in children using many of the same or similar assessment tools used for adults. Identifying OCD in young children presents a unique challenge, however, because children learn about the world around them through rituals and repetition. Children believe in magic and incorporate magical beliefs into rules of behavior. So when does "Step on a crack, break your momma's back" become a symptom of OCD and not just a kid trying to make sense of an absurd world? There's no easy answer to this question, but mostly it comes down to how unhappy your child seems when the rules are inevitably broken. Does your child have a meltdown if she can't avoid stepping on cracks? While stepping over cracks, does your child seem relaxed and curious, or does she seem disturbed and conflicted?

Keep in mind that even ideas your child may have no real understanding of, such as sexual ones, can be fodder for obsessions.

Common Obsessions and Compulsions in Young Children

Contamination OCD

- Excessive concern with germs, especially after learning about them at school

- Excessive focus on getting sick, especially in response to kids at school getting sick (possibly accompanied by emetophobia, an obsessive fear of vomiting)

Just Right OCD

- Excessive concern with order and numbers

- Superstitious fears gone too far (for example, panicking at stepping on a crack in the sidewalk)

- Urges to touch or tap items or to repeat behaviors to achieve a certain feeling

Harm OCD

- Obsessive fear of parents dying

- Intrusive upsetting thoughts about parents getting harmed

- Self-harm fears and fears of being harmed by others (especially fear of home invasion)

OCD with sexual obsessions

- Intrusive sexual thoughts about family members, combined with confessing and reassurance-seeking

- Fear of having behaved sexually

- Sexual orientation fears (often socially anxious concerns about being labeled "gay" by peers)

Religious obsessions

- Excessive concern with blasphemous thoughts or following religion the "right" way

- Fear of cosmic retribution (may originate from upsetting stories in religious doctrine)

Moral obsessions

- Excessive guilt after misbehaving or breaking a perceived rule

- Dependence on confessing and apologizing to function (for example, refusing to eat, get dressed, or do other basic tasks unless you respond to a question about morality or hear a confession about a "bad thought")

Externalize the OCD

The notion that all people have unwanted thoughts—that being aware of an intrusive image of your parents dying because you failed to ritualize the right way, for example, doesn't reflect real danger—is too overwhelming for most children to tolerate. Thus when trying to help your child with OCD, it's important to portray the OCD as an outside agitator. When your child can say: "It's not me. It's my OCD," or "OCD is *in* me. OCD is not *me*," it removes any guilt and shame and places it on the real culprit, the OCD.

A good starting point is to collaborate with your child on a suitable name for the OCD—for example, the Big Bug (or Dr. Spikesalot, or Meanzilla). Then promote the view that your child doesn't *want* to do compulsions, but the Big Bug demands them. The Big Bug likes to give him a hard time, but there are things he can do to help put the monster in its place. Talking about the OCD as though it's a creature that resides inside your child's mind places you in an alliance with your child against the OCD. From this standpoint, your efforts to invite change and reduce accommodation are less likely to be viewed as threats and more likely to be viewed as battle strategies against Count Snotula.

Accommodations

Children are very likely to request accommodation of their symptoms, and their rapidly developing and adaptable brains make them fast learners. They'll quickly pick up on the fact that accommodation reduces their discomfort, so they'll do whatever it takes to get it. If your child has OCD, I recommend you review part 2 of this book, paying particular attention to chapter 6, "When Your Family Member Is Seeking Reassurance." Denying reassurance to anyone you care about is extremely challenging, but denying reassurance to your young child can bring up immense guilt and fear of being an inadequate or insensitive parent. Keep in mind that a good parent does whatever it takes to protect a child from harm. Don't lose sight of what's causing the harm: fight the OCD, not your guilt.

Once your child has been diagnosed with OCD, it's of utmost importance that you reduce and eliminate accommodation as soon as possible. Though no doubt well-intentioned (you want to relieve your child's distress), accommodation complicates family dynamics and ultimately impairs your child's ability to learn how to master the anxiety associated with the OCD. Accommodation also keeps your child from seeing that feared consequences (for example, "I'll get sick if I touch that") fail to occur (Storch et al. 2007). If you've been accommodating the OCD for a long time, don't stop all at once, but know that ongoing accommodation of young children with OCD is likely to cause additional problems. For example, if your child is demanding that you shower before touching the TV remote, and you've been complying, then she may fail to develop an appropriate respect for other people's autonomy. This can lead to conflict with peers and an increasing sense of entitlement and disrespect for authority figures such as teachers, babysitters, and of course you. These types of issues could prove just as damaging to her relationships and functioning overall as the OCD itself.

Discipline

Your young child with OCD may be driven to engage in compulsive behaviors that violate family rules at times. Let's say he refuses to eat from a plate that you've touched because you didn't wash your hands the way the "OCD says" you're supposed to. Negotiating without accommodating his compulsive avoidance won't be easy. But if he takes the plate and throws it across the room, there's more going on than just OCD.

I'm not saying you should discipline your child for doing compulsions. And you wouldn't want to take an authoritarian approach to parenting, because this is associated with greater symptoms (Timpano et al. 2010). But you won't serve your child well unless you reinforce appropriate behavior. If your child needs to be disciplined, be understanding and patient while providing structure and consequences. Be careful to make it clear you're not disciplining her for her OCD or her personality, but disciplining her for her *actions*. If you have two or more children, treat them fairly and consistently—be sure not to give your child with OCD special treatment or special kinds of discipline.

Be Yourself

Maintaining your sense of self can help you cope when any family member has OCD, but it may be most important when parenting a young child with OCD. Parenting a child with OCD is distressing on multiple levels. You may be weighed down with concern over whether your child will be able to function at school, in a job, or in a relationship (Storch et al. 2009). OCD has a way of sucking all the energy out of daily experiences. Your child's OCD may quickly become the center of attention and, quite naturally, you may find yourself fixating on trying to get this disorder out of your child, out of your family. However, in addition to learning about OCD and how to address it, your young child is also learning about you, who you are, what you expect as a parent, and what your values mean. Remember the four I's from chapter 4? The fourth one is "Integrate and model healthy behavior." Your integrating and modeling healthy behavior for your young child is essential to his forming both a healthy identity and a healthy view of you. So be careful not to become just the "OCD dad" or "OCD mom," as if you were just an extension of his OCD.

Dos and Don'ts for Supporting
Your Young Child with OCD

Do	Don't
Speak openly and confidently about OCD with your child, emphasizing that the condition is treatable and without shame.	Assume that your child's OCD behaviors are defiant or the result of poor discipline, or punish your child for doing compulsions.
Frame getting professional help as a sign of strength, and help your child access cognitive-behavioral treatment and psychiatric evaluation.	Act as though you're your child's therapist, or create exposures "on the spot" (not developed with a therapist).
Educate your child's school or other caregivers about OCD.	Pressure your child to "get over it" or to get "better" faster.
Give your child praise and rewards for standing up to her OCD, whether her efforts are successful or not.	Assign blame to your partner or to your other children for your child's OCD, or try to make anyone feel guilty that there's OCD in your family.
Refer to the OCD as a separate entity (for example, "the Bully"), and encourage an open dialogue about what the OCD is saying.	Point out the negative, what isn't being worked on, or what "failures" you catch. Also, don't criticize how other caregivers (for example, your child's other parent) handle the OCD in front of your child.
Normalize therapy as "learning to fight the Bully."	Hover near your child to watch for compulsions.
Present a unified front with other caregivers (for example, your child's other parent) in how treatment is reinforced.	Attempt to force your child to go to therapy if she doesn't want to.

When Your Adolescent Child Has OCD

Many OCD symptoms peak shortly before or during puberty. Changes in hormones, rapid brain development, and changes in academic and social expectations all likely play a role. To make matters worse, the OCD now has far more material to work with. Though it's not unusual for young children to struggle with thoughts of a violent or sexual nature, such thoughts are more likely to occur in adolescents. This may stem partly from increased exposure to violent or sexual material in media (such as video games), which expands the library of mental images, but is more likely due to a burst in growth in areas of the brain responsible for sex and aggression, combined with new social interactions that bring the potential for violence and sexual behavior. But sexual or violent obsessions aren't the only obsessions that may pop up during adolescence. The increased pressure for academic performance can coincide with increased compulsive perfectionism (rereading, rewriting, excessive checking, and other behaviors), which may actually interfere in functioning at school. Young people may be particularly prone to dreading mistakes and dreading being *seen* having made mistakes by their peers, resulting in increased perfectionism and compulsive attempts to achieve flawlessness (Ye, Rice, and Storch 2008).

The transition from childhood to adulthood is a confusing and often painful time. Your adolescent child wants autonomy and independence, but she still depends on you for food and shelter. She wants to have her voice heard—a voice she only recently developed—but adults control all the podiums. Parenting an adolescent with OCD means taking an aggressive enough stance to help your child address the disorder (including helping her access professional treatment), but remaining distant enough that you don't deprive her of much-needed empowerment and independence. It can be especially challenging. Parents of adolescents with OCD are more likely to struggle with mental health problems of their own and rely more heavily on coping strategies such as avoidance (Derisley et al. 2005).

Common OCD Issues That May Become Visible in Adolescence

Adolescents who already show signs of Contamination OCD may find their symptoms worsening as they encounter a wider variety of triggering concepts and simultaneously learn more about them (for example, harmful chemicals, bodily fluids, and diseases). As social pressure to "fit in" increases, the concept of "emotional contamination," a fear of becoming or transforming into an undesirable person or "type" of person, may occur. This can result in a lot of avoidant behavior as the adolescent OCD sufferer tries not to dress like certain people, sit near certain people, or have specific thoughts about certain people.

Increased academic demands at this age may also lead to school perfectionism and obsessive concern with exactness, symmetry, or accuracy of written work, leading both to procrastination of schoolwork and to excessive time spent doing that same schoolwork. The arrival of new responsibilities (for example, this is *your* locker, your school book, your keys) may lead to hyper-responsibility (checking) OCD issues in a susceptible adolescent. As puberty and exposure to increasingly violent and sexual concepts coincide, adolescents may struggle with increasingly vivid violent and sexual intrusive thoughts. Fear of negative evaluation by peers and the natural confusing feelings that come with puberty may exacerbate fears of being the "wrong" sexual orientation or being deviant in any way. Early romantic relationships may lead to obsessive concern over "love feelings" and whether those feelings are the right kind or the right way. Religious and moral scrupulosity may get worse as religious concepts are studied further and better understood and expectations to comprehend morality increase.

Discipline

When your children are young, it's important that you present yourself as authoritative yet loving, directive yet nurturing. Discipline can be a challenge for any parent, but parenting an adolescent with OCD has unique challenges. Your adolescent child with OCD may regress into childlike behavior (for example, throwing tantrums or feigning helplessness) to manipulate you into providing reassurance or other accommodations. Or he may choose to punish you by isolating himself in his room and refusing to communicate. Or he may act out by drinking, using drugs, or engaging in other risky behaviors.

It's essential that your child with OCD not come to believe that your love is conditional on his ability to control or manage the OCD. As he ages, this will become even more critical. As his ability for abstract thinking grows, so too will his ability to blame you for ruining his life! (Though my six-year-old has already accused me of "ruining her life" for running out of popcorn on movie night.) Still, this is the time when you should experience a different kind of pushback from your kids. Parenting an adolescent with OCD doesn't mean letting him get away with everything. But it does mean being clear about when and why privileges may be taken away, something that should *not* be tied to the presence of OCD symptoms.

There is one exception to this guideline. If your adolescent child is in treatment or working on his OCD, he may invite you to hold him accountable to doing his OCD homework by using incentives. Welcome this invitation with open arms. Incentives such as tickets to a concert for a few weeks of consistent effort can be very motivating. On the other hand, punishments, such as removal of phone or computer privileges, for failure to work on the OCD are likely to contribute only to defiance and continued compulsive behavior.

Support

Trust me, your adolescent child wants your support. She just doesn't want to be *seen* wanting it. She needs to believe that you believe she can do things on her own. If she feels as if she's being shuffled off to a therapist to be "fixed" or as if she's being marginalized as "the sick one" in the family, she'll mold herself to that role. She knows her OCD better than you do, and for that she deserves some respect and some autonomy in dealing with it. The key for you as her parent is to be available to support her battle against the disorder without being overinvolved.

Adolescents may want support, but they don't want empathy unless it's genuine. Something about the rapidly developing teenage brain makes them excel at sniffing out false praise and lip service. If you don't get what it's like to be a teen with OCD, admit it—first to yourself and then to your child. If he gets upset about something that doesn't seem like a big deal—and he will—don't tell him how *you'd* handle it. You'll get a better response if you admit you don't know what he's going through (but offer to help in any way you can) than if you imply he's just being dramatic.

People in general typically don't want to think of themselves as sick, weird, or "mentally ill," and the pressure to fit in or be otherwise accepted among peers may be highest during adolescence. Your child may feel self-hatred as a result of being diagnosed (or self-diagnosed) with OCD. The line of thinking may be something like: *I just now started figuring out who I am in this crazy world. Turns out I'm crazy. Something's wrong with me. I'm not wired right.* The trick to effectively parenting an adolescent with OCD is walking that line between normalizing the OCD experience ("You're not crazy; you just have OCD") and emphasizing the importance of acknowledging the OCD ("This is a real problem, and you really do need to address it").

Dos and Don'ts for Supporting
Your Adolescent Child with OCD

Do	Don't
Express a desire to understand your child's OCD, but concede that you're old and can't really understand what it's like to be young anymore.	Assume that your child's OCD behaviors are defiant, the result of poor discipline, or "just a phase."
Encourage cognitive-behavioral treatment or psychiatric evaluation in a nonjudgmental way, being sensitive to concerns your child may have about the stigma of getting treatment and his desire to keep the OCD private from peers.	Talk about your child's OCD in mixed company without his approval.
Present a unified front with other caregivers (for example, your child's other parent) in how treatment is reinforced.	Attempt to guide your child through therapy.
Give your child adequate space and privacy.	Pressure your child to "get over it" or to get "better" faster.
Educate your child's teachers or other caregivers about OCD.	Punish your child for doing compulsions.
Give your child praise and rewards for standing up to OCD, whether her efforts are successful or not.	Assign blame to your child's other parent or to your other children for the OCD.
Encourage the use of a teen OCD support group (online, or in person when available).	Characterize everything your child does as OCD behavior.

When Your Adult Child Has OCD

As family members grow and age, they go through various shifts in roles and responsibilities. In early adulthood, children are expected to leave the house (often to go to college), get a job, get married, and so on. But it's a scary world out there. There are many reasons for "failure to launch," and OCD is a common one. Your adult child with OCD may leave home but still be functionally impaired, dependent on you to accommodate the OCD and perhaps reliant on you financially. "Failure to launch" can be a significant stressor for a family.

Having an adult child with OCD may mean you have to cope with some painful realities about her future limitations and her expectations. You may experience a lot of guilt or doubt about your child's prospects. Did you get her enough help? Did you give her enough resolve to accept the help and fight her OCD? There are no simple or easy answers to such questions, but there's one cold truth: the answers don't change the situation. Your child can be thirty or forty and still need the same help you would have, could have, or even *should* have given her to fight the disorder.

Supporting your adult child with OCD often starts with taking an inventory of what interventions have taken place. If you've already done everything you can think of, but nothing seems to have worked, more aggressive interventions may play an important role. For example, if your child is already on medication for OCD, it may be useful to consult with the prescribing doctor about changing dosages or augmenting psychiatric approaches with additional medications. Increasing the intensity of outpatient therapy to intensive outpatient or residential programs may be warranted.

Adults with OCD aren't more likely to have any particular type of obsession than children with OCD. However, they may be more likely to have depression or social phobia if their functioning has been long impaired by OCD. For this reason, if you're providing housing and financial support for your adult child because he's seemingly incapable of taking care of himself, consult with an OCD treatment professional before making any significant shifts in accommodations of such a broad nature. Because your child may have started buying into the distorted belief that he's incapable of functioning, it might set off a crisis that could lead to suicidality, self-harm, or other unsafe behaviors.

Adults with OCD who rely on their parents for financial support often already feel a lot of guilt and shame. Rather than try to use guilt as a motivator by complaining about all the sacrifices you continue to make, use "support and belief" language instead. For example, "I know this OCD has been a nightmare for you, but I still believe you can come out on top if you push yourself and do the work." Don't throw it in your child's face that you expected to stop paying for his rent by now. He knows. Your choices are to stop the accommodation and take the risk that he'll never get better (or may even get worse) or continue the accommodation and encourage treatment. Complaining while continuing to accommodate is passive-aggressive and will only create anger and shame.

College and OCD

Obsessive-compulsive and anxiety disorders are relatively common in college students but often go undiagnosed because the symptoms may be confused with being distracted or unmotivated or because shame keeps sufferers from seeking help (Sulkowski, Mariaskin, and Storch 2011). If your child with OCD is away at college, it may be difficult for you to ascertain how she's doing. Visiting her often, if possible, may be better than relying on phone calls or e-mails. College-aged OCD sufferers are likely to isolate themselves and withhold unhappy information from their family. Your college student with OCD may still be feeling pressure from her teenager mind to "not be a crazy" and "not need her parents" on top of pressure to "be independent" and "take care of business." As a supportive parent, you may need to remember the limits of your ability to control the situation from afar. This again highlights the importance of self-care. If your child is struggling with OCD at college, coming home to healthy parents will mean a lot to her.

Dos and Don'ts for Supporting Your Adult Child with OCD

Do	Don't
Express a desire to understand your child's OCD, but be careful not to compete with him over "who knows the most."	Criticize or mock your child's symptoms—be especially conscious of speaking condescendingly or treating her in an age-inappropriate manner.
Encourage cognitive-behavioral treatment or psychiatric evaluation in a nonjudgmental way, and help your child access treatment.	Try to use guilt as a motivator for change by bringing up the sacrifices you have made to support your child.
Encourage independence, employment, and social interaction.	Allow concern for your child to define your every waking moment.
Encourage the use of an OCD support group (online, or in person when available).	Smother your child with constant check-ins and expressions of your worry about him.
Stay in regular but not too frequent contact with your child, so that you can monitor symptoms when needed.	Use therapy as a bargaining chip against continued support.

When Your Sibling Has OCD

This book is primarily geared toward adult readers. Many of those who stand to benefit the most from this section on siblings with OCD (and the following section on parents with OCD) may be too young to understand or appreciate it. If you're an adult, consider ways in which you can articulate what you learn here to your younger family members who may need it most.

If you have a sibling with OCD, it's inevitable that you'll get a confusing amount of attention at home. Sometimes you'll get less attention than you deserve, because your brother or sister's OCD is stealing the limelight. Sometimes you'll get more attention than you want, because your parents feel guilty about often focusing all of their attention on your sibling with OCD. You have a challenging path to navigate. On one hand, you need to make some space for your sibling to take the attention he needs. You have to make sacrifices that can seem unfair, such as being late to an event because of traffic on the way back from your sister's therapy appointment. Or you may find yourself having to make sacrifices more directly tied to your sibling's OCD because the family as a whole is continuing to accommodate her. Suddenly there are rules about who can touch what, and if you break them, your parents freak out and yell at you, even though the rules are stupid and make no sense. On the other hand, you can't keep giving and giving without ending up resentful of your sibling with OCD. So you have to assert your needs. You have to tell your parents if you need more attention or less.

Your sibling with OCD may struggle with a number of interactions with you. If she has contamination fears, there may be obsessive concern that objects you have touched have been contaminated, or she may be concerned with contaminating you in some way or causing you illness. Just Right OCD may generate compulsive urges to touch or physically bother you in some way in order to feel right. You may be the focus of unwanted obsessive violent or sexual thoughts, resulting in avoidance and excessive concern over any kind of touching or interaction.

Psychological Effects of OCD on Siblings

Parents may grossly underestimate the psychological toll it takes on a child when she's told that *she* must behave strangely in order to keep her "strange" sister from falling apart. The pressure to keep the sibling with OCD whole, safe, and sane is more than any child should have to endure. Such *parentification* of a child (being placed in a caregiving role primarily reserved for parents) may result in long-term psychological harm, because increased parentification correlates with increased mental health issues in adulthood (Jankowski et al. 2013).

You may end up believing yourself to be more "broken" than your sibling with OCD, especially if you're constantly scolded for breaking family rules that exist around the OCD (rules that you now know only perpetuate the obsessive-compulsive cycle). This creates a systemic problem within a systemic problem. The family system is already running on a deficit, because the OCD's demands only get worse the more they're accommodated. Now you feel resentment, resulting in reduced support of your sibling with OCD but not reduced accommodation, worsening the OCD and increasing the role OCD plays in the family. Following are some common sacrifices made by brothers and sisters of people with OCD:

- Losing time with the sibling and/or with parents who are devoted to the OCD

- Following rules laid down by the sibling with OCD (or by the parents) that are designed to accommodate compulsions

- Receiving negative feedback from parents for failing to accommodate the sibling with OCD

- Not being the "special" one with the "problem"

A Special Relationship

Sibling relationships are complex and can range from fully enmeshed (having no boundaries between each other) to completely disengaged (wanting nothing to do with each other). This is obviously going to affect how you relate to your sibling's OCD. But perhaps *you* can be the one to educate your sibling (or educate your parents, for that matter) about OCD and accommodation. Rather than antagonize your sibling, try to form an alliance with him. Let him know you see the difference between him and his OCD. "Mom and Dad are doing their best, but they don't get it. I know you, bro. I miss you. How can I get you back?" If you don't have OCD, you won't know what it's like to deal with the obsessions and compulsions that burden your sibling, but you do know what it's like to be your parents' child. Nobody but you and your sibling know what that's like, and this type of shared experience and empathy can set the stage for a level of compassion and understanding that will really make a difference.

Dos and Don'ts for Supporting Your Sibling with OCD

Do	Don't
Express a desire to understand your sibling's OCD, but be sensitive to your sibling's desire for privacy and refrain from prying.	Use your sibling's OCD as a weapon in conflict, or compare yourself to your sibling to make him feel bad.
Attempt to engage your sibling in activities you'd both enjoy regardless of the OCD.	Blame your sibling's OCD for personal or family problems.

Assert your needs to your parents, but remember they may already be doing the best they can or may not realize how hard it is for you.	Use negative or dangerous behaviors to compete for your parents' attention.
Let your sibling know you're on her side in the fight against OCD.	Sabotage gains your sibling has made in treatment, or go out of your way to trigger your sibling's OCD as a form of punishment.

When Your Parent Has OCD

If you have a parent with OCD, it probably seems as though nobody knows what you really go through. Sure, other people watch their parents fight. But your parents fight over what seem like the most ridiculous things. Plus, you have to live by special rules that nobody else has. Don't touch this, don't say these words, don't mention that topic, and try to keep Dad from noticing this or try to keep Mom from encountering that.

In the previous section, I mentioned the problem with parentification. Nowhere is this more problematic than in the case of a child or teen living with a parent who has OCD. Very often, the child is forced into the position of caregiver. That may mean walking on eggshells to avoid upsetting the parent with OCD, or it may mean acting as a surrogate spouse and providing emotional support to the other parent. When a parent has OCD, kids commonly have to deal with:

- Feelings of insecurity, abandonment, and self-blame when the parent's OCD results in avoidance

- Fear of what might trigger the parent's OCD next

- Loss of respect for the parent if the parent doesn't attempt to get better

- Jealousy of families unburdened by OCD

- Resentment toward the other parent for not standing up to the parent with OCD and for allowing the OCD to run the household

- Being late for school or events due to having to wait for the parent to do compulsions

- Special rules that make no sense

- Parental marital conflict caused by the OCD

- Feelings of inadequacy for not being able to fix the parent with OCD

- Fear of becoming just like the parent with OCD

- Feelings of embarrassment around the parent with OCD in social situations

Living with a parent with OCD presents a number of challenges, including conflict in the relationship with the parent with OCD, the pressure of caring for the parent, concerns about stigma, and fears about getting OCD from the parent (Griffiths et al. 2012).

Common Obsessions and Compulsions That Affect How Parents Treat Their Children

Contamination OCD

- Concern that children are contaminated, leading to avoidance of bathing or touching children

- Compulsive urges to ask children to wash themselves or their possessions or to ask them to avoid touching certain things
- Fear of getting children sick by spreading contaminants

Harm OCD

- Fear of murdering or abusing children
- Avoiding being alone with children for fear of causing harm
- Fear of poisoning children with food or other contaminants

Hyper-responsibility (checking) OCD

- Excessively checking on children to ensure their safety
- Demanding that children participate in checking rituals

OCD with sexual obsessions

- Unwanted intrusive thoughts or images that sexualize children
- Fear of becoming sexually attracted to children

Relationship OCD

- Fear of not loving children enough or the right way
- Fear of being seen as a bad parent

Religious or moral scrupulosity

- Excessive attention to "perfect" parenting
- Excessive attention to being sure that children have adopted important cultural or religious beliefs
- Fear of feeding, dressing, or educating children in some imperfect way

The Avoidant Parent

Parents with OCD may avoid certain kinds of interactions with their children because they trigger obsessive thoughts. A father with sexual obsessions may compulsively avoid giving his child a bath, or a mother with contamination fears may avoid playing with her child in the communal sandbox. But parents with OCD may often also try to avoid certain kinds of interactions with their children only because they might trigger an *emotion* that could lead to obsessive thoughts.

For example, a mother with Harm OCD may avoid disciplining her child when he misbehaves because she's trying to avoid experiencing anger, which may trigger the violent thoughts she fears. Or a father with unwanted sexual obsessions may avoid interacting with his daughter on even the most basic level. His train of thought might go: *If I ask how her day at school was, she'll tell me about what she learned. I'll then feel proud of her, which will make me feel love for her. My love feelings will trigger an urge to analyze my feelings to make sure that the feelings have no sexual connotation. I might even have some kind of groinal response and will get stuck obsessing about that. It's better to just avoid her altogether.*

In some ways, this *emotional avoidance* can be even more damaging to families than physical avoidance, because the causes are so hard to pinpoint and because the children may be more likely to conclude that they're simply unloved. Both in traditional CBT and in "third-wave" CBT approaches, such as dialectical behavioral therapy (DBT) and acceptance and commitment therapy (ACT), there's an emphasis on highlighting personal values, such as "being an effective parent," as motivation for reducing such avoidance. Children of parents with OCD don't have many options for reminding their parents of these values, other than attempting to get their attention. Such attempts may be healthy, such as inviting the parent to participate in fun activities, or unhealthy, such as engaging in risky behaviors.

It's Not Your Fault

The most important thing to remember is that the situation in your family is not your fault. You didn't cause your parent's OCD. You're not making it worse, and you're not the one who can make it better either.

Your job is to simply be a constant for your parent with OCD. People who struggle with OCD struggle with fear, anxiety, and change. By just being yourself, you can be one less variable for your parent to contend with. That being said, don't let your parent's OCD control you any more than it has to. Assert your needs as best you can. If neither of your parents is willing to address the OCD, reach out to a teacher or someone you trust. In rare cases, severe OCD can lead to neglect and emotional abuse of children, which needs to be addressed and reported (such as in cases where children's freedom of movement or nutrition is being affected by OCD rules that have spun out of control).

Dos and Don'ts for Supporting Your Parent with OCD

Do	Don't
Express a desire to understand your parent's OCD, but give him space, because sharing mental health issues with one's child can feel shaming.	Blame yourself or accept blame for triggering your parent's OCD.
Be vocal about the burden your parent's OCD places on you.	Act as though you're your parent's therapist, or assert authority over your parent because of her OCD.

Attempt to engage your parent in activities you'd both enjoy regardless of the OCD, but give your parent time to readjust to activities she has previously avoided because of OCD.	Sabotage gains your parent has made in treatment, or go out of your way to trigger your parent's OCD as a form of punishment.
Assert your needs to both of your parents.	Use negative or dangerous behaviors to compete for attention.

When Anyone Has OCD

It wouldn't be feasible to include a section in this book for every possible relationship affected by OCD. I've covered the most common ones, but OCD affects cousins, nephews and nieces, aunts and uncles, stepparents, girlfriends and boyfriends, roommates, and coworkers too. Your family is whatever you define your family as. More to the point, a person's OCD can affect not only the people she interacts with, but also the people *they* interact with. Perhaps you have a best friend whose child has been diagnosed with OCD. Watching your friend cope, strategize, suffer, and complain—that's not easy either. What I'd like you to take away from this chapter is that you need to meet the person in pain—the OCD sufferer—wherever she is and support and encourage her to get whatever help she can, while maintaining healthy boundaries and a healthy sense of who *you* are to her. You're not her therapist, and when you put emphasis on "fixing" or "therapizing" the ones you love instead of on simply loving, supporting, and learning about them, communication breaks down and the system falls apart. So whatever relationship you share with someone with OCD, or whichever dynamic in this book resonates with you the most, aim to step away from judgment and criticism and move toward empathy and trust.

Chapter 11

Family Trip
(to the Waiting Room)

When a family seeks treatment for any kind of mental disorder, they're essentially inviting an outside person (the mental health care provider) to take a temporary (and sometimes not-so-temporary) role in the family dynamic. Furthermore, mental health care treatment for OCD often involves at least two outside people: a cognitive-behavioral therapist and a psychiatrist. It may also involve other mental health care providers, physicians, teachers, and more. We pay these people with money, but we also pay them with trust. Some forms of family therapy view the therapist as entering the family itself, becoming part of the system, and enabling change from the inside. Trusting someone from outside the family to enter and make changes in the family system costs anxiety. It costs the willingness to accept that the family cannot address the problem on their own. The returns on this investment can be unpredictable. When it doesn't work out—if, for example, your family member receives an unhelpful form of psychotherapy or is prescribed ineffective medications—the family may be left in worse shape than before. When it does work out, words do little justice to the relief that the family experiences as a result of receiving quality mental health care. In this chapter, I hope to help you maximize the likelihood of a successful return on your investment.

Treatment Providers

Most commonly, your family member will first seek the help of either a psychotherapist or a psychiatrist. This decision will be based on a combination of factors, including whether your family member views the problem as primarily a chemical imbalance (and thus seeks medication first) or a psychological imbalance (and thus seeks therapy first). Other factors may include financial issues, health insurance issues, and the accessibility of specialists in your geographical area.

Psychiatrists

A psychiatrist is a medical doctor (MD) who specializes in the medical treatment of mental health issues and is capable of prescribing medication for those issues. To be a psychiatrist, you need extensive education and training: college, medical school, a clinical internship, and a residency. The process is even longer for those who specialize in child psychiatry.

Historically the role of the psychiatrist was to handle all aspects of mental health care, but in the last few decades, changes in managed care have resulted in psychiatrists frequently being responsible just for medication management, whereas psychotherapists (see below) address other aspects of treatment.

When possible, it's best to work with a psychiatrist who has extensive experience working with OCD sufferers. Though psychiatrists have a responsibility to learn about the latest medical and psychotherapeutic treatments, they may be less likely to stay up-to-date on treatments for disorders they don't have much experience with. A good way to increase the likelihood of working with a suitable psychiatrist, then, is to ask lots of questions about his experience treating OCD. You may want to begin your search using the list of treatment providers at the website of the International OCD Foundation (http://www.iocdf.org).

If you're seeking treatment for your adolescent or young child, keep in mind that you'll be having a lot of contact with the psychiatrist you choose, perhaps even more than your child will, so it's especially important to locate a suitable one. You may wish to educate yourself on the role medication can play in treating OCD (see chapter 3) and act as an intermediary between the psychiatrist and your child. The key thing to remember is to ask lots of questions.

Dos and Don'ts When Your Family Member Is Seeking/Seeing a Psychiatrist

Do	Don't
Have an open discussion with your loved one about medication.	Tell your loved one to take (or not take) medication. (You can encourage compliance with the psychiatrist's recommendations, but never coerce your loved one, even your child.)
Help seek out a psychiatrist with extensive experience in OCD and related disorders.	Assume that all psychiatrists are the same.
Educate yourself on the role of medication in treating OCD.	Demand that the psychiatrist prescribe your loved one a particular medication.
Ask the psychiatrist questions about medication side effects, dosages, and expected outcomes.	Make psychiatric decisions for your loved one.

Psychotherapists

A psychotherapist is someone who is trained in diagnosing mental disorders and using therapeutic techniques for treating those disorders. In order to be a licensed psychologist, you need a doctorate in psychology (PhD or PsyD), but other psychotherapists qualified to treat OCD may include licensed MFTs (marriage and family therapists), LCSWs (licensed clinical social workers), and LPCCs (licensed professional clinical counselors). Different states may use slightly different names for these licenses.

The psychotherapist is the mental health care provider with whom your loved one, and perhaps you and the rest of your family, will likely have the closest relationship. The best treatment approach available for OCD is cognitive-behavioral therapy, or CBT (see chapter 3). Finding a CBT specialist in your area can be difficult, however. To determine whether someone is truly competent to treat OCD, you'll want to ask (or encourage your family member with OCD to ask) some specific questions:

- "Do you specialize in CBT?"

  This is a different question from "Can you do CBT?" Though many therapists have no training in CBT, most have had at least some exposure to it in their studies. People seeking treatment for OCD should look for therapists who truly specialize in CBT.

- "How much of your practice focuses on OCD?"

  Consider that research on OCD continues at a rapid pace, making it unlikely that a therapist who sees only the occasional OCD sufferer will be up-to-date on and well-versed in implementing the best techniques.

- "Do you use exposure with response prevention (ERP)?"

  Though some competent therapists in the OCD treatment community may downplay ERP or place a greater emphasis on mindfulness, all therapists who treat OCD competently will use some form of ERP. Most therapists specializing in OCD will employ both ERP and mindfulness strategies. Therapists who rely primarily on relaxation techniques, eye movement desensitization and reprocessing (EMDR), or traditional talk therapy are less likely to effectively treat OCD.

There are certainly other questions worth asking, but these are likely the most important for determining which mental health care providers might be able to truly help your family member with OCD.

The Therapeutic Relationship

Sometimes a therapist becomes so much a part of the family system that he loses objectivity and may find himself participating in family rituals that perpetuate the problem. This is what you might see with a therapist who offers excessive reassurance about obsessions. Cognitive-behavioral therapists should inhabit the role of coach and educator. The therapist should be a part of the family system, but at the same time operate independently from it, providing information about the disorder, insight into problematic behaviors, and directives to change those behaviors.

As the supportive family member, contemplate what kind of relationship is appropriate for you to have with your loved one's therapist. Do you want to have unrestricted access to the therapist, a lot of feedback, and a lot of correspondence with the therapist between sessions? Or would you prefer a more distant relationship, akin to the one you might have with your loved one's car mechanic? Most likely something in between is best. If your loved one is an adult, she'll decide your level of involvement, but setting realistic expectations at the outset may help her in making this decision.

If your young child has OCD, you and the therapist will be collaborators, forming a coalition against the OCD and inviting your child to join you. This coalition will be strengthened by your ability to reinforce the therapist's recommendations at home. If your adolescent child has OCD, you'll have a similar job, but you'll also need to provide some space for your young one to develop more skills for fighting OCD independently. This may mean you'll need to "back off" sometimes and trust that the therapist and your child are connecting. Maintaining your distance is even more important when supporting an adult family member with OCD.

Remember that accommodation worsens OCD, in part because it sends the message to the sufferer that he's incapable of choosing to resist compulsions. This chips away at his self-confidence and self-esteem and leads to hopelessness in the face of the disorder. Becoming overinvolved in your loved one's therapy can be a form of accommodation, wherein you perpetually *give* him the skills instead of letting him learn the skills. One way to instill the opposite message, that your family member is capable, is to leave some of the therapy in his hands.

For example, if you helped your family member find a therapist, now give your family member space and time to do the work. This doesn't mean you can't ask questions or shouldn't be involved in treatment at all; in fact, you may be a regular part of treatment, especially if your family member's obsessions directly involve you. But *she* should be the one to decide how much contact you'll have with her therapist. Use the tools discussed in part 2 of this book to help inform you of how involved to be, and pay particular attention to how you invite collaboration in addressing the problem.

Dos and Don'ts When Your Family Member Is Seeking/Seeing a Therapist

Do	Don't
Have an open discussion with your loved one about seeking CBT.	Present getting psychotherapy as a last-ditch effort or a form of giving up.

Help your loved one seek out a therapist with extensive experience in OCD and related disorders.	Assume that all therapists who say they treat OCD or do CBT are sufficiently qualified.
Educate yourself on CBT for OCD and on the role you can play in your loved one's therapy.	Pressure your loved one to get better, or pressure the therapist to "fix" your loved one.
Ask the therapist questions (with your loved one's consent) about treatment and when to get involved versus when to promote independence.	Come up with your own CBT or ERP approaches for your loved one without the advice of the therapist.

Treatment Intensity

Figuring out what level or intensity of treatment is best for your family member may take a little research. After administering a professional assessment, a trained treatment provider should be able to determine roughly how severe the OCD is and what the ideal treatment environment might be. For those who cannot access or afford professional help, self-help CBT workbooks may be the best resource available (see the resources at the end of this book).

Outpatient treatment. Regular outpatient treatment of OCD consists of one-on-one sessions with a CBT therapist, typically once a week (for roughly an hour) over the course of several months, with a gradual reduction in frequency until there's only the occasional "booster" session. Sessions may be more than once a week in the beginning or during times of increased symptom severity. Sessions will most commonly take place in the therapist's office, but some may take place over the phone or via video chat. OCD specialists will often facilitate exposures outside of the office as well, which may occasionally mean meeting at different locations.

Recent studies suggest that exposure-based CBT treatment specifically involving structured work with the family can reduce symptom severity and impairment, including the role of accommodation (Piacentini et al. 2011). In some instances, couple-based CBT may be warranted. A recent study found the couple-based program developed by Jon Abramowitz and colleagues at the University of North Carolina to be very effective in reducing symptoms of OCD, depression, and relationship issues in long-term couples (Abramowitz et al. 2013). In other words, your role in your family member's treatment will benefit you as well.

Intensive and residential treatment. Severe OCD may need more intensive treatment. Your family member may want to look into an intensive outpatient program that provides CBT several days a week. Even more intensive treatment may include a residential program of several weeks or months of daily therapy. The word "intensive" is subject to interpretation, however, so you'll need to look closely at the program description. Quality intensive programs will typically involve not only longer or more frequent sessions but also medication management, group therapy, and a clinical team approach.

If you go this route, the sheer number of treatment providers involved in your family member's struggle can seem overwhelming. Many intensive programs include family therapy or support groups designed to address this and to maximize treatment at every level.

Group therapy. Group CBT can also be useful, so long as the severity of your family member's OCD is not so high as to interfere in her participation. If your family member with OCD has a co-occurring personality disorder (for example, borderline personality disorder), group treatment may not be appropriate, because the symptoms of that disorder may interfere in communicating with other group members or be exacerbated by the group environment. Though your family member would have to divide her treatment time with others, being around people who "get it" and are doing the same hard work with CBT and ERP can be extremely motivating.

Finding the Right Support for Yourself

There's a reason flight attendants tell passengers to put on their own oxygen mask first in the event of a sudden loss of cabin pressure: you need to be well in order to help someone in need. This doesn't mean that everyone who has a family member with OCD needs professional help, but there's no prize for going it alone, and you owe it to yourself to have some form of support. Parents who have strong emotional resources tend to feel less burdened by caring for an OCD child (Storch et al. 2009), and the benefit of strong emotional resources may be the same for anyone caring for someone with OCD.

There's support aimed at fostering a better understanding of the OCD, and then there's self-care. In terms of the former, you may be able to find a local support group for family members of OCD sufferers; as of this writing, however, such groups are rare. There are also a few online groups and discussion boards specifically for family members (see the resources at the end of the book). Most intensive and residential OCD programs include some amount of family therapy and family-supportive therapy. In some cases, you might have sessions with your family member's therapist even without your family member present (with your family member's permission, of course).

In terms of self-care, you may benefit from your own individual therapy. Coping with a family member who suffers from any illness is challenging, but both the ongoing symptoms and the treatment of OCD itself can be taxing (for example, if your family member is doing ERP, symptoms often get worse before they get better). A therapist who is trained in relational dynamics and stress management may be able to help you process your feelings about the OCD and the role it plays in your family.

We all have issues. You may or may not have OCD, but you certainly have your own unique challenges. If you can address them in therapy, it may be helpful to both you and your family member with OCD. For example, you may have a history of not feeling capable of asserting yourself in challenging situations because of experiences you had growing up. Without therapy, you may be more likely to cave to your family member's demands for accommodation, resulting in a worse outcome for both of you.

When you're healthy, you're more likely to be present and supportive of the health of your loved ones. Staying healthy means taking care of your body and taking care of your mind. Too often, family members of people with OCD find themselves sacrificing everything to help the ones they love. But sacrificing your wellness won't help your family member with OCD. What will help is displaying healthy behavior that makes the OCD behavior more obvious and more separate from your family member, leading your family member to greater insight and a greater capability to fight back.

Consider This

OCD is a painful, frustrating, and—above all—isolating disorder. It can cause people to crumble under the weight of their own thoughts, become slaves to their compulsions, and leave their loved ones in the dark. I don't struggle with OCD the way I used to, but I still have to remind myself from time to time that not everyone thinks the same way I do. My wife and kids remind me, too: my wife does so simply by being a constant, nonjudgmental presence; my kids, by running around firmly grounded in the present moment.

My OCD doesn't bring me down anymore, but it does pull me aside from time to time. That's when I have to remain aware: Oh, right, that's just how I think. Acknowledging that everything I have of value in my life today I have because of my continued efforts to master my OCD helps me stay committed.

Your Struggle

You actually read this whole book? You must really love your family member with OCD. It would be so easy to just leave her behind, to not care, to let the OCD take her down. But you won't stand for it. You won't let this disorder steal your loved one from you.

In chapter 1, I suggested you consider why you were reading this book. The answer, I'm sure you found, is because nothing will stop you from keeping your loved one with OCD in your life. Any tip, any piece of advice you picked up in these pages is another weapon in your family's fight against OCD. And when your family system comes together to battle OCD, the system will evolve: your family will grow closer, more cherished, and more reliable than ever.

Acknowledgments

This book would not have been possible without the support and efforts of New Harbinger acquisitions editor Jess O'Brien, who, when I wrote him to update my mailing address, asked if I wanted to write another book about OCD. I would also like to thank the entire New Harbinger editorial team for never allowing me to steer too far off course in guiding this ship to its final destination. I owe a debt of gratitude to Lindsey Bergman, John Piacentini, Erika Nurmi, and Tara Peris at the UCLA Child OCD, Anxiety and Tic Disorders Program, for their guidance and expertise when I worked in their intensive outpatient clinic and met so many amazing and inspiring families with OCD. Thanks to Jonathan Grayson for his friendship and mentorship over the years and to Wendy Mueller for her support and encouragement. Most importantly, I'd like to thank my own family, both the one I was born to and the one I created. Both have taught me about unconditional acceptance of loved ones, which I've come to believe is the only environment in which people can truly grow.

Resources

Websites

International OCD Foundation:

https://www.iocdf.org (see especially https://iocdf.org/expert-opions/family-issucs/)

Anxiety and Depression Association of America:

http://www.adaa.org

Association for Behavioral and Cognitive Therapies:

http://www.abct.org

Beyond OCD:

http://www.beyondocd.org

Books

For a more comprehensive list of relevant books, visit the International OCD Foundation's web page http://www.iocdf.org /books.

Books for Family Members of OCD Sufferers

Landsman, K. J., K. M. Rupertus, and C. Pedrick. 2005. *Loving Someone with OCD: Help for You and Your Family*. Oakland, CA: New Harbinger Publications.

March, J. S. 2006. *Talking Back to OCD: The Program That Helps Kids and Teens Say "No Way"—and Parents Say "Way to Go."* New York: Guilford Press.

Wagner, A. P. 2002. *What to Do When Your Child Has Obsessive-Compulsive Disorder: Strategies and Solutions*. Rochester, NY: Lighthouse Press.

Books About OCD/Self-Help Workbooks

Abramowitz, J. S. 2009. *Getting Over OCD: A 10-Step Workbook for Taking Back Your Life*. New York: Guilford Press.

Baer, L. 2002. *The Imp of the Mind: Exploring the Silent Epidemic of Obsessive Bad Thoughts*. New York: Plume.

Grayson, J. 2014. *Freedom from Obsessive-Compulsive Disorder: A Personalized Recovery Program for Living with Uncertainty*. Updated ed. New York: Berkley.

Hershfield, J., and T. Corboy. 2013. *The Mindfulness Workbook for OCD: A Guide to Overcoming Obsessions and Compulsions Using Mindfulness and Cognitive Behavioral Therapy*. Oakland, CA: New Harbinger Publications.

Hyman, B., and C. Pedrick. 2010. *The OCD Workbook*. 3rd ed. Oakland, CA: New Harbinger Publications.

Penzel, F. 2000. *Obsessive-Compulsive Disorders: A Complete Guide to Getting Well and Staying Well*. New York: Oxford University Press.

Online Discussion Boards

Everything OCD:

http://www.facebook.com/everythingOCD

OCD-Support:

http://groups.yahoo.com/neo/groups/OCD-Support/info

The OCD and Parenting List:

http://groups.yahoo.com/neo/groups/ocdandparenting/info

The Parents of Adults with OCD List:

http://groups.yahoo.com/neo/groups/parentsofadultswithocd/info

Parents of Teens and Young Adults with OCD:

http://groups.yahoo.com/neo/groups/OCD-POTAYA/info

References

Abbey, R. D., J. R. Clopton, and J. D. Humphreys. 2007. "Obsessive-Compulsive Disorder and Romantic Functioning." *Journal of Clinical Psychology* 63 (12): 1181–92.

Abramowitz, J. S., D. H. Baucom, S. Boeding, M. G. Wheaton, N. D. Pukay-Martin, L. E. Fabricant, C. Paprocki, and M. S. Fischer. 2013. "Treating Obsessive-Compulsive Disorder in Intimate Relationships: A Pilot Study of Couple-Based Cognitive-Behavior Therapy." *Behavior Therapy* 44 (3): 395–407.

Aksaray, G., B. Yelken, C. Kaptanoglu, S. Oflu, and M. Özaltin. 2001. "Sexuality in Women with Obsessive Compulsive Disorder." *Journal of Sex & Marital Therapy* 27 (3): 273–77.

American Psychiatric Association. 2007. *Practice Guideline for the Treatment of Patients with Obsessive-Compulsive Disorder.* Arlington, VA: Author.

————. 2013. *Diagnostic and Statistical Manual of Mental Disorders, Fifth Edition.* Arlington, VA: Author.

Barrett, P., A. Shortt, and L. Healy. 2002. "Do Parent and Child Behaviours Differentiate Families Whose Children Have Obsessive-Compulsive Disorder from Other Clinic and Non-clinic Families?" *Journal of Child Psychology and Psychiatry* 43 (5): 597–607.

Beucke, J. C., J. Sepulcre, T. Talukdar, C. Linnman, K. Zschenderlein, T. Endrass, C. Kaufmann, and N. Kathmann. 2013. "Abnormally High Degree Connectivity of the Orbitofrontal Cortex in Obsessive-Compulsive Disorder." *JAMA Psychiatry* 70 (6): 619–29.

Black, D. W., G. R. Gaffney, S. Schlosser, and J. Gabel. 2003. "Children of Parents with Obsessive-Compulsive Disorder—A 2-Year Follow-Up Study." *Acta Psychiatrica Scandinavica* 107 (4): 305–13.

Bloch, M. H., J. McGuire, A. Landeros-Weisenberger, J. F. Leckman, and C. Pittenger. 2010. "Meta-analysis of the Dose-Response Relationship of SSRI in Obsessive-Compulsive Disorder." *Molecular Psychiatry* 15 (8): 850–55.

Boeding, S. E., C. M. Paprocki, D. H. Baucom, J. S. Abramowitz, M. G. Wheaton, L. E. Fabricant, and M. S. Fischer. 2013. "Let Me Check That for You: Symptom Accommodation in Romantic Partners of Adults with Obsessive-Compulsive Disorder." *Behaviour Research & Therapy* 51 (6): 316–22.

Calvocoressi, L., C. M. Mazure, S. V. Kasl, J. Skolnick, D. Fisk, S. J. Vegso, B. L. Van Noppen, and L. H. Price. 1999. "Family Accommodation of Obsessive-Compulsive Symptoms: Instrument Development and Assessment of Family Behavior." *Journal of Nervous & Mental Disease* 187 (10): 636–42.

Charles, R. 2001. "Is There Any Empirical Support for Bowen's Concepts of Differentiation of Self, Triangulation, and Fusion?" *American Journal of Family Therapy* 29 (4): 279–92.

Chödrön, P. 1991. *The Wisdom of No Escape: And the Path of Loving-Kindness.* Boston, MA: Shambhala Publications.

Cisler, J. M., R. E. Brady, B. O. Olatunji, and J. M. Lohr. 2010. "Disgust and Obsessive Beliefs in Contamination-Related OCD." *Cognitive Therapy & Research* 34 (5): 439–48.

Cougle, J., A. Goetz, K. Hawkins, and K. Fitch. 2012. "Guilt and Compulsive Washing: Experimental Tests of Interrelationships." *Cognitive Therapy & Research* 36 (4): 358–66.

Craske, M. G., K. Kircanski, M. Zelikowski, J. Mystkowsi, N. Chowdhury, and A. Baker. 2008. "Optimizing Inhibitory Learning During Exposure Therapy." *Behaviour Research and Therapy* 46 (1): 5–27.

Derisley, J., S. Libby, S. Clark, and S. Reynolds. 2005. "Mental Health, Coping and Family-Functioning in Parents of Young People with Obsessive-Compulsive Disorder and with Anxiety Disorders." *British Journal of Clinical Psychology* 44 (3): 439–44.

Fairfax, H. 2008. "The Use of Mindfulness in Obsessive Compulsive Disorder: Suggestions for Its Application and Integration in Existing Treatment." *Clinical Psychology & Psychotherapy* 15 (1): 53–59.

Foa, E. B. 2010. "Cognitive Behavioral Therapy of Obsessive-Compulsive Disorder." *Dialogues in Clinical Neuroscience* 12 (2): 199–207.

Franklin, M. E., J. S. Abramowitz, M. J. Kozak, and E. B. Foa. 2000. "Effectiveness of Exposure and Ritual Prevention for Obsessive-Compulsive Disorder: Randomized Compared with Nonrandomized Samples." *Journal of Consulting and Clinical Psychology* 68 (4): 594–602.

Gomes, J. B., B. Van Noppen, M. Pato, D. T. Braga, E. Meyer, C. F. Bortoncello, and A. V. Cordioli. 2014. "Patient and Family Factors Associated with Family Accommodation in Obsessive-Compulsive Disorder." *Psychiatry and Clinical Neurosciences* 68 (8): 621–30.

Goodman, W., L. H. Price, S. A. Rasmussen, C. Mazure, R. L. Fleischmann, C. L. Hill, G. R. Heninger, and D. Charney. 1989. "The Yale-Brown Obsessive Compulsive Scale Part I. Development, Use, and Reliability." *Archives of General Psychiatry* 46 (11): 1006–11.

Greenberg, B. D., M. Altemus, and D. L. Murphy. 1997. "The Role of Neurotransmitters and Neurohormones in Obsessive-Compulsive Disorder." *International Review of Psychiatry* 9 (1): 31–44.

Griffiths, J., E. Norris, P. Stallard, and S. Matthews. 2012. "Living with Parents with Obsessive-Compulsive Disorder: Children's Lives and Experiences." *Psychology & Psychotherapy: Theory, Research & Practice* 85 (1): 68–82.

Haghighi, M., L. Jahangard, H. Mohammad-Beigi, H. Bajoghli, H. Hafezian, A. Rahimi, H. Afshar, E. Holsboer-Trachsler, and S. Brand. 2013. "In a Double-Blind, Randomized and Placebo-Controlled Trial, Adjuvant Memantine Improved Symptoms in Inpatients Suffering from Refractory Obsessive-Compulsive Disorders (OCD)." *Psychopharmacology* 228 (4): 633–40.

Hershfield, J., and T. Corboy. 2013. *The Mindfulness Workbook for OCD: A Guide to Overcoming Obsessions and Compulsions Using Mindfulness and Cognitive Behavioral Therapy*. Oakland, CA: New Harbinger Publications.

Jankowski, P. J., L. M. Hooper, S. J. Sandage, and N. J. Hannah. 2013. "Parentification and Mental Health Symptoms: Mediator Effects of Perceived Unfairness and Differentiation of Self." *Journal of Family Therapy* 35 (1): 43–65.

Kellner, M. 2010. "Drug Treatment of Obsessive-Compulsive Disorder." *Dialogues in Clinical Neuroscience* 12 (2):187–97.

Leonard, R. C., and B. C. Riemann. 2012. "The Co-Occurrence of Obsessions and Compulsions in OCD." *Journal of Obsessive-Compulsive and Related Disorders* 1: 211–5.

March, J., A. Frances, D. Carpenter, and D. Kahn. 1997. "The Expert Consensus Guideline Series: Treatment of Obsessive-Compulsive Disorder." *Journal of Clinical Psychiatry* 58 (s4): 1–72.

Mattheisen, M., J. F. Samuels, Y. Wang, B. D. Greenberg, A. J. Fyer, J. T. McCracken, et al. 2015. "Genome-Wide Association Study in Obsessive-Compulsive Disorder: Results from the OCGAS." *Molecular Psychiatry* 20 (3): 337–44.

McDougle, C. J., W. K. Goodman, J. F. Leckman, and L. H. Price. 1993. "The Psychopharmacology of Obsessive-Compulsive Disorder: Implications for Treatment and Pathogenesis." *Psychiatric Clinics of North America* 16 (4): 749–66.

McKay, D., J. Piacentini, S. Greisberg, F. Graae, M. Jaffer, J. Miller, F. Neziroglu, and J. A. Yaryura-Tobias. 2003. "The Children's Yale-Brown Obsessive-Compulsive Scale: Item Structure in an Outpatient Setting." *Psychological Assessment* 15 (4): 578–81.

Murray, C. J., and A. D. Lopez. 1996. *The Global Burden of Disease: A Comprehensive Assessment of Mortality and Disability from Diseases, Injuries, and Risk Factors in 1990 and Projected to 2020.* Cambridge, MA: Harvard University Press.

Nakatani, E., G. Krebs, N. Micali, C. Turner, I. Heyman, and D. Mataix-Cols. 2011. "Children with Very Early Onset Obsessive-Compulsive Disorder: Clinical Features and Treatment Outcome." *Journal of Child Psychology & Psychiatry* 52 (12): 1261–68.

Nestadt, G., J. Samuels, M. Riddle, O. J. Bienvenu III, K. Y. Liang, M. LaBuda, J. Walkup, M. Grados, and R. Hoehn-Saric. 2000. "A Family Study of Obsessive-Compulsive Disorder." *Archives of General Psychiatry* 57 (4): 358–63.

Olatunji, B. O., M. L. Davis, M. B. Powers, and J. A. Smits. 2013. "Cognitive-Behavioral Therapy for Obsessive-Compulsive Disorder: A Meta-analysis of Treatment Outcome and Moderators." *Journal of Psychiatric Research* 47 (1): 33–41.

Piacentini, J., R. L. Bergman, S. Chang, A. Langley, T. Peris, J. J. Wood, and J. McCracken. 2011. "Controlled Comparison of Family Cognitive Behavioral Therapy and Psychoeducation/Relaxation Training for Child Obsessive-Compulsive Disorder." *Journal of the American Academy of Child and Adolescent Psychiatry* 50 (11): 1149–61.

Pittenger, C., B. Kelmendi, M. Bloch, J. H. Krystal, and V. Coric. 2005. "Clinical Treatment of Obsessive Compulsive Disorder." *Psychiatry (Edgmont)* 2 (11): 34–43.

Przeworski, A., L. Zoellner, M. Franklin, A. Garcia, J. Freeman, J. March, and E. Foa. 2012. "Maternal and Child Expressed Emotion as Predictors of Treatment Response in Pediatric Obsessive-Compulsive Disorder." *Child Psychiatry & Human Development* 43 (3): 337–53.

Pujol, J., C. Soriano-Mas, P. Alonso, N. Cardoner, J. M. Menchón, J. Deus, and J. Vallejo. 2004. "Mapping Structural Brain Alterations in Obsessive-Compulsive Disorder." *Archives of General Psychiatry* 61 (7): 720–30.

Radomsky, A. S., G. M. Alcolado, J. S. Abramowitz, P. Alonso, A. Belloch, M. Bouvard, et al. 2014. "You Can Run but You Can't Hide: Intrusive Thoughts on Six Continents." *Journal of Obsessive-Compulsive and Related Disorders* 3 (3): 269–79.

Rasmussen, S. A., and J. L. Eisen. 1992. "The Epidemiology and Clinical Features of Obsessive Compulsive Disorder." *The Psychiatric Clinics of North America* 15: 743–58.

———. 1997. "Treatment Strategies for Chronic and Refractory Obsessive-Compulsive disorder." *Journal of Clinical Psychiatry* 58 (Suppl 13): 9–13.

Renshaw, K. D., G. Steketee, and D. L. Chambless. 2005. "Involving Family Members in the Treatment of OCD." *Cognitive Behaviour Therapy* 34 (3): 164–75.

Rotge, J. Y., A. H. Clair, N. Jaafari, E. G. Hantouche, A. Pelissolo, M. Goillandeau, et al. 2008. "A Challenging Task for Assessment of Checking Behaviors in Obsessive-Compulsive Disorder." *Acta Psychiatrica Scandinavica* 117 (6): 465–73.

Rotge, J. Y., D. Guehl, B. Dilharreguy, J. Tignol, B. Bioulac, M. Allard, P. Burbaud, and B. Aouizerate. 2009. "Meta-Analysis of Brain Volume Changes in Obsessive-Compulsive Disorder." *Biological Psychiatry* 65 (1): 75–83.

Samuels, J., and G. Nestadt. 1997. "Epidemiology and Genetics of Obsessive-Compulsive Disorder." *International Review of Psychiatry* 9 (1): 61–72.

Sasson, Y., J. Zohar, M. Chopra, M. Lustig, I. Iancu, and T. Hendler. 1997. "Epidemiology of Obsessive-Compulsive Disorder: A World View." *Journal of Clinical Psychiatry* 58 (Suppl. 12): 7–10.

Skapinakis, P., T. Papatheodorou, and V. Maureas. 2007. "Antipsychotic Augmentation of Serotonergic Antidepressants in Treatment-Resistant Obsessive-Compulsive Disorder: A Meta-analysis of the Randomized Controlled Trials." *European Neuropsychopharmacology* 17 (2): 79–93.

Starcevic, V., D. Berle, V. Brakoulias, P. Sammut, K. Moses, D. Milicevic, and A. Hannan. 2011. "The Nature and Correlates of Avoidance in Obsessive-Compulsive Disorder." *Australian & New Zealand Journal of Psychiatry* 45 (10): 871–79.

Steinhausen, H. C., C. Bisgaard, P. Munk-Jørgensen, and D. Helenius. 2013. "Family Aggregation and Risk Factors of Obsessive-Compulsive Disorders in a Nationwide Three-Generation Study." *Depression and Anxiety* 30 (12): 1177–84.

Steketee, G., and B. Van Noppen. 2003. "Family Approaches to Treatment for Obsessive Compulsive Disorder." *Journal of Family Psychotherapy* 14 (4): 55–71.

Stengler, K., S. Olbrich, D. Heider, S. Dietrich, S. Riedel-Heller, and I. Jahn. 2013. "Mental Health Treatment Seeking Among Patients with OCD: Impact of Age of Onset." *Social Psychiatry & Psychiatric Epidemiology* 48 (5): 813–19.

Stewart, S. E., Y. P. Hu, D. M. Hezel, R. Proujansky, A. Lamstein, C. Walsh, et al. 2011. "Development and Psychometric Properties of the OCD Family Functioning (OFF) Scale." *Journal of Family Psychology* 25 (3): 434–43.

Storch, E. A., G. R. Geffken, L. J. Merlo, M. L. Jacob, T. K. Murphy, W. K. Goodman, M. J. Larson, M. Fernandez, and K. Grabill. 2007. "Family Accommodation in Pediatric Obsessive-Compulsive Disorder." *Journal of Clinical Child & Adolescent Psychology* 36 (2): 207–16.

Storch, E., H. Lehmkuhl, S. Pence, G. Geffken, E. Ricketts, J. Storch, and T. Murphy. 2009. "Parental Experiences of Having a Child with Obsessive-Compulsive Disorder: Associations with Clinical Characteristics and Caregiver Adjustment." *Journal of Child & Family Studies* 18 (3): 249–58.

Sulkowski, M. L., A. Mariaskin, and E. A. Storch. 2011. "Obsessive-Compulsive Spectrum Disorder Symptoms in College Students." *Journal of American College Health* 59 (5): 342–48.

Taylor, S. 2013. "Molecular Genetics of Obsessive-Compulsive Disorder: A Comprehensive Meta-analysis of Genetic Association Studies." *Molecular Psychiatry* 18 (7): 799–805.

Thompson-Hollands, J., A. Edson, M. C. Tompson, and J. S. Comer. 2014. "Family Involvement in the Psychological Treatment of Obsessive-Compulsive Disorder: A Meta-analysis." *Journal of Family Psychology* 28 (3): 287–98.

Timpano, K. R., M. E. Keough, B. Mahaffey, N. B. Schmidt, and J. Abramowitz. 2010. "Parenting and Obsessive Compulsive Symptoms: Implications of Authoritarian Parenting." *Journal of Cognitive Psychotherapy* 24 (3): 151–64.

Torres, A. R., N. T. Hoff, C. R. Padovani, and A. T. Ramos-Cerqueira. 2012. "Dimensional Analysis of Burden in Family Caregivers of Patients with Obsessive-Compulsive Disorder." *Psychiatry & Clinical Neurosciences* 66 (5): 432–41.

Waters, T. L., and P. M. Barrett. 2000. "The Role of the Family in Childhood Obsessive-Compulsive Disorder." *Clinical Child & Family Psychology Review* 3 (3): 173–184.

Williams, M. T., and S. G. Farris. 2011. "Sexual Orientation Obsessions in Obsessive-Compulsive Disorder: Prevalence and Correlates." *Psychiatry Research* 187 (1–2): 156–59.

Williams, M. T., S. G. Farris, E. Turkheimer, A. Pinto, K. Ozanick, M. E. Franklin, M. Liebowitz, H. B. Simpson, and E. B. Foa. 2011. "Myth of the Pure Obsessional Type in Obsessive-Compulsive Disorder." *Depression and Anxiety* 28 (6): 495–500.

Ye, H. J., K. G. Rice, and E. A. Storch. 2008. "Perfectionism and Peer Relations Among Children with Obsessive-Compulsive Disorder." *Child Psychiatry & Human Development* 39 (4): 415–26.

Yoshida, T., C. Taga, Y. Matsumoto, and K. Fukui. 2005. "Paternal Overprotection in Obsessive-Compulsive Disorder and Depression with Obsessive Traits." *Psychiatry & Clinical Neurosciences* 59 (5): 533–38.

Jon Hershfield, MFT, is a psychotherapist who specializes in mindfulness-based cognitive behavioral therapy (MBCBT) for obsessive-compulsive disorder (OCD) and related disorders, and is licensed in the states of Maryland and California. He is director of The OCD and Anxiety Center of Greater Baltimore in Hunt Valley, MD, and coauthor of *The Mindfulness Workbook for OCD*. Hershfield is a frequent presenter at the annual conferences of both the International OCD Foundation and the Anxiety and Depression Association of America, and a professional contributor to multiple online support groups for OCD.

Foreword writer **Jeff Bell** is an author, health advocate, and radio news anchor. His two books, *Rewind, Replay, Repeat* and *When in Doubt, Make Belief*, have established Bell as a leading voice for mental health awareness and "Greater Good" motivation. Bell serves as a national spokesperson for the International OCD Foundation. In 2011, he cofounded the nonprofit A2A Alliance (http://a2aalliance.org), aiming to showcase and foster the power of turning adversity into advocacy. Bell is a twenty-year veteran of broadcast news and currently coanchors the KCBS Afternoon News, winner of the 2014 Edward R. Murrow Award for Best Newscast in America.

FROM OUR PUBLISHER—

As the publisher at New Harbinger and a clinical psychologist since 1978, I know that emotional problems are best helped with evidence-based therapies. These are the treatments derived from scientific research (randomized controlled trials) that show what works. Whether these treatments are delivered by trained clinicians or found in a self-help book, they are designed to provide you with proven strategies to overcome your problem.

Therapies that aren't evidence-based—whether offered by clinicians or in books—are much less likely to help. In fact, therapies that aren't guided by science may not help you at all. That's why this New Harbinger book is based on scientific evidence that the treatment can relieve emotional pain.

This is important: if this book isn't enough, and you need the help of a skilled therapist, use the following resources to find a clinician trained in the evidence-based protocols appropriate for your problem. And if you need more support—a community that understands what you're going through and can show you ways to cope—resources for that are provided below, as well.

Real help is available for the problems you have been struggling with. The skills you can learn from evidence-based therapies will change your life.

Matthew McKay, PhD
Publisher, New Harbinger Publications

**If you need a therapist, the following organization
can help you find a therapist trained in cognitive behavioral therapy (CBT).**
The Association for Behavioral & Cognitive Therapies (ABCT) Find-a-Therapist service offers a list of therapists schooled in CBT techniques. Therapists listed are licensed professionals who have met the membership requirements of ABCT and who have chosen to appear in the directory.
Please visit www.abct.org and click on *Find a Therapist*.

**For additional support for patients, family, and friends,
please contact the following:**
International OCD Foundation (IOCDF)
Visit www.ocfoundation.org

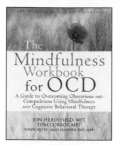

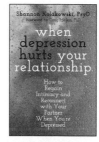